D1796561

Kestrels In The Kitchen

Kestrels In The Kitchen

The Story of Bob and Pat Ratcliffe

as told to

Meg Elizabeth Atkins

W. H. ALLEN . London
A Howard & Wyndham Company
1979

Copyright © Meg Elizabeth Atkins, 1979

This book or parts thereof may not be
reproduced without permission in writing

Printed and bound in Great Britain by
REDWOOD BURN LIMITED,
Trowbridge & Esher
for the publishers W. H. Allen & Co. Ltd,
44 Hill Street, London W1X 8LB

ISBN 0 491 02247 6

Contents

Illustrations

Photographs numbered 1–6, 8–12, 14 are by Enid Michael; 7, 16 by *Sunday Express*, Manchester; 13, 15, 17 by Peter Cowgill.

Prologue

The fishing hawk had been on a long and dreadful journey. Someone, in an attempt to smuggle her into the country, had hacked off her feathers to reduce her size and packed her into a tiny box without food or water. This box, in its turn, was concealed in a false compartment of another box. How long she had suffered this confinement, where she had come from or where she was illegally bound for were questions my wife Pat and I did not ask when we took charge of her. We were concerned with the creature as she was, scarcely alive and almost demented by her experience; the essential was to bring her back to health, everything else was irrelevant.

With the minimum of delay the fishing hawk passed from the hands of the airport authorities to the police. She was put into a tea-chest and driven on the last stage of her journey, through the autumn evening to our small house on the outskirts of Manchester.

Jeannie, the fishing hawk, had come home.

One

The bird people

Home: a terraced house in a narrow street, the front door opens on to the pavement, the back door to a small yard; we're hemmed in by a maze of streets of identical houses, frowned on distantly by high rise flats. An unexpected place, I admit, to find an assortment of birds – owls, kestrels, gulls, buzzards, geese, ducks, mynahs. Cats, too, which according to the rules do not form alliances with birds, much less make gentle and interested companions for them. But I've spent my life caring for birds, I've done it my way, and if the rules don't fit I ignore them.

I can't remember the first time I held a bird in my hand, first felt the miracle of its construction, the downy warmth of its body, the strength of its wings. It must have been over forty years ago when I was a child and we lived in Chorlton-cum-Hardy, south of Manchester where the wandering course of the river Mersey marked the edge of the town. Beyond it the country began.

Where we lived the houses were all the same shape and all the same colour and the quiet streets with their neat gardens went down gradually to the fields. It was very peaceful there. I remember waking on spring mornings, so early there was no light in the sky, and feeling the quiet stretching out all around me, hearing the owls call eerily as they hunted through the dawn. Their haunting cries died away one by one and I would think: *they've gone home to sleep now.* The silence stole back, but not for long. Just as the first light began to pale the darkness somewhere, distant and clear, a bird began to sing . . . then another . . . and another . . . until the whole world was full of

11

their song.

Of course, there were birds at home, family pets – budgies, and one day there was a sparrow. I don't know where it came from or why it adopted us, it just always seemed to be there, so I suppose I accepted as absolutely natural the fact that a wild thing should choose to make its home with human beings.

When the sparrow wanted to travel about it tucked itself under the collar of my mother's coat and went out with her. Indoors, it lived in a vase on the sideboard; most of the time it flew or hopped about, playing with the budgies when they were out of their cage, but if the sparrow was nowhere in sight I knew where to look for it. We used to put old bits of string in the vase until a whole jumble of it had accumulated; the sparrow must have come upon this one day and found that as it was dark and quiet and cosy it made an ideal nest. Whenever I wanted to find him I only had to look in there and see his bright little eyes glinting up at me through the gloom.

As soon as I was old enough to go out on my own I began to explore the river bank. In those days the country was open, farmland and marshland where Wythenshawe housing and industrial estates stand now. The fields on either side of the river are low and have always flooded in rainy weather. It was bleak there in winter, a sombre landscape with bare trees and hedges black as etchings under leaden skies. But in summer the winding, dusty track of Hawthorn Road was bordered by the hedges from which it took its name and they were clustered – for miles, it seemed – with white blossoms that gave off a dense, heavy scent; in sunlight the river lay like a dark green glass, reflecting the foliage of the trees and the high grass on its banks. The Bridgewater Canal stood high over the fields, stretching from the rural villas of Brooklands and Sale, through Chorlton, straight into the heart of that dark industrial wilderness, Trafford Park.

But if you turned your back on the factories and houses you could walk a long way without meeting anything very much. Baguley hospital had been built, apart from that there were only fields stretching out to a collection of corrugated iron shacks that was Manchester Airport. But it wasn't the few

12

planes that interested me, it was the birds: goldfinches, bullfinches, skylarks, blackbirds, herons and ducks – because this was before the Mersey became polluted and there were plenty of waterfowl to watch there, and there were swallows and swifts skimming over the river, jackdaws in the spinneys and rooks calling harshly from their tree-tops.

I was observant, as all children are, with an eye for detail. If I saw a bird I didn't recognise I worried and wondered, asking questions where I could. I don't recall ever having any nature lessons at school, I suppose we did, but they never told me what I wanted to know, so I had to seek another source of information. And I found it – books. The local library, presents – if I was lucky – or pocket money hoarded with miserly determination. When I wasn't watching birds – bad weather never put me off but the short winter days or illness did – I could read about their life-cycles, their habits, their anatomy. I wasn't interested much in reading about anything else – the pleasure of reading for its own sake came later to me – and there was no television to distract, or inform, and visits to the cinema were few.

For years my only companion of these riverside excursions was our family dog. He had come from a neighbouring farm as a grown dog so we never knew how old he was; he was called Bob, too. He was a cross between an old English sheepdog and a bull terrier, a strange enough sight, and he weighed over eight stone. He was gentle enough with me but he was not disposed to be friendly to anything in the dog line and many a local dog, pitching in for the hell of it, learnt to respect his size and his battling terrier blood.

As long as I had Bob I was perfectly content to be without human company, and I preferred to be alone rather than spend my time with someone who didn't share and so couldn't appreciate my interest in wild life. But then, in the chance and undefined ways of solitary children, I fell into the company of a labourer who worked on a nearby farm. I began by stopping to have a word with him, then accompanying him as he went about his work; very soon I was spending every spare moment helping him about the farm – after school, weekends and holidays, all year round.

I thought of him as old Patrick but maybe he wasn't really so old, to a child anyone over twenty-five is ancient. He had the effortless knowledge of livestock and natural history true to every countryman. He was not a talkative man, probably not even very friendly, but he just accepted me and took it for granted that, as I was his companion, I should know what he knew, and he opened my eyes to what was going on around me.

We could be tramping along a cart track in the quiet of the day and he could point to a piece of ground I might have inattentively been looking at and say, 'See – that partridge chick?' And sure enough, I'd see the smudgy brown little thing where before I had seen nothing. He showed me a jackdaw perched on the back of a sheep stealing scraps of wool to make a lining for its nest. Delicately trodden pathways I never knew existed he pointed out to me as the runs of foxes; because he knew the area all around and that most foxes have their own gateways he would guess exactly where to look.

It was in his company that I saw wild mallards for the first time. There was a pond on the farm where I often fished but never, in all the quiet hours I'd spent there, did I realise that the mallards were nesting close at hand. The hen sits in absolute stillness on a nest built in the reeds, so cunningly camouflaged it is virtually invisible, and I must have passed one particular nest a hundred times without being aware of it. But Patrick had noticed, just in the course of his daily work, the direction in which she occasionally flew backwards and forwards and knew exactly where we could find her.

Like all countrymen he could poach. In the conditions of the time this was not a daring enterprise, undertaken for the hell of it, it was necessity. Old Patrick lived in a tied cottage with his wife and numerous children and he earned fifty shillings a week to keep them all. He came from generations of farm workers and he, like them, had to learn to live off the land; an occasional hare or pheasant made a much-needed addition to their meagre diet. I never questioned the morality of this and I'm sure he never did. He and his kind were scrupulously honest in their dealings with people, they laboured long, hard hours for very

14

little return, the simplest amenities were rare in their lives and luxury unknown; but they worked close to the earth, its labour was theirs. Its bounty, too.

Ever since, as a boy, I've kept and cared for birds I have had to accept the fact of death. I have had to acknowledge that there are times when I can do nothing, but there are other times when, against all the odds, an apparently crippled bird will recover and happily live out its natural life-span.

At first, it cost me a great deal of heartache coming across an injured bird I had neither the means nor the skill to help; there was never any doubt I had to do *something*, although this instinct was for many years frustrated by my inexperience. I consulted books whenever possible, and I had Patrick to go to for advice, but I had no money to pay vets' fees or buy first aid equipment or medicines. I could rear orphaned fledgelings and I successfully mastered the technique of mending broken legs and wings. Such help as I could give, by its very simplicity, seemed hopelessly inadequate to me; but I knew it was what I must do, I knew it was all I could do, and for a while that had to be enough.

I walked down the tree-lined lane to Wynstay House in a state of awe and excitement I would have died rather than let anyone suspect. It was the first day of my first job. I was going to work as an apprentice at Flatters and Garnett, a firm of laboratory and scientific instrument makers.

Naturally, to my innocent eye, everyone on their way to work that morning looked purposeful, important and sure of themselves. I was so overwhelmed by the strangeness of leaving my schooldays behind and entering the real world that I walked more and more slowly, dawdling at the entrance to Wynstay House, and had to jump for my life as a merry, brown-haired girl on a bicycle skidded past me with a shout of 'Watch where you're going, idiot!'

I gathered my dignity as best I could and saw her flying figure disappear round the side of the building. I'd have given anything, at that moment, for a share of her assurance, her gaiety.

15

'I'll remember you,' I gloomed to myself, full of envy. I wondered what her name was and later asked someone.

'Pat,' I was told. 'She works in the lab and she's cycling mad.'

Cycling, in my scale of interests, came way behind birds, but then, so did everything. Working in the laboratory, in an atmosphere of examination and enquiry, handling the tools that were to form the groundwork of my career in engineering, prompted me to do some enquiring on my own behalf.

Every time I gave successful treatment to an injured bird I learnt something. I realised that the unsuccessful attempts had a part in the pattern of things, too; those small, pathetic corpses were not just failures, they were a means of teaching me far more than any textbook ever could. So, whenever a bird died, instead of asking myself why? what went wrong? – I dissected it in order to try to find the answer for myself. It is a practice I've kept up to this day – when necessity demands or time permits. Over the years Pat and I have gradually extended our knowledge so that, if someone gave us every single bone from the skeleton of a bird – and there are over two hundred – and mixed them all up, I think we could put them together again in the right order.

I hadn't been working very long at Flatters and Garnett before I got to know Pat. I reminded her that she had nearly run me over on my first day. 'So I did,' she said, and taking my remark to indicate a passion for bicycles, told me about the club to which she belonged. They met every weekend at Cheadle Green, which in those days before the by-pass was built really was a village green; she suggested that if I had nothing to do some time I might like to go out for a run with them. It seemed a good idea and I agreed and so came to discover the pleasure of exploring Derbyshire and Cheshire with the cycling club. And, of course, I got to know Pat, our friendship progressing gradually to courtship, the bond between us slowly strengthening in our shared love of birds.

In Pat's home, as in mine, there had always been budgies – plus cats, goldfish, a tortoise and a dog. Pat had an instinct for caring for animals, it wasn't sentimental or unrealistic, it had all the practical elements essential to her job as a laboratory technician. 'After all,' she said to me in her sensible way, 'I spend most of my time surrounded by things pickled in bottles.'

Side by side with this entirely commonsense approach there was always that natural, caring impulse that prompted her to respond to any creature in need of help. When anyone at work found a bird or small animal orphaned or injured, they took it to Pat, and she often says her recollection of those times is the countless hours she spent chewing up bread and cake to push into the beaks of fledgelings.

Working together, spending our leisure together, our interest in birds grew in a way we scarcely noticed. It wasn't something we worked at or made any conscious effort to develop, it was simply part of ourselves, part of our lives; it had always been there in both of us as separate individuals, in time it became our life together.

When we married we went to live with Pat's parents. My dog Bob was then getting to be a great age, it didn't seem fair to move him from the home he'd known so long. Apart from the business of getting him accustomed to a strange place while we were both out at work all day, there was also the problem of Rusty, the little Sheltie that had been Pat's family pet for years.

Rusty wasn't going to have any strange dog usurping her place in the house – much less in anyone's affections, she'd already made that clear to Bob and, less than half his size, bullied him ferociously. She got away with it, partly, I think, because of Pat. My dog had never been very keen on human beings much – except me and my family – but he took to Pat the instant he met her. He was very possessive and inclined to guard her with unnecessary devotion, he even warned me off once or twice, to her amusement. I think it was for her sake, in a spirit of great sacrifice, he tolerated the snappy little Sheltie, but the prospect of trying to maintain the peace between them in a house that wasn't our own was a little too daunting.

We decided it would be best for Bob to stay with my family until we got our own place, but before that happened the old boy became ill with dropsy and had to be put down. He'd had a good long life, eighteen years with us so God knows how old he really was, and I'd never have seen him suffer at the end of it. But I felt a wrench at his going, we'd shared a lot in the way two loners can, sometimes, in the years of my growing up.

Shortly after we were married I bought Pat a budgie as an Easter present. Her family's bird had died a little while before and the cage in the kitchen seemed to both of us to be just waiting for a new occupant. One bird of our own wasn't enough for me, though, and one day when we were out shopping in Manchester we went to Tib Street. Twenty years ago this narrow side-street in the heart of the town was lined with pet shops of every description. In the years I've lived here it has seemed to me that Manchester has been pulled down crashing about my ears and a totally unrecognisable place constructed; it's a matter of amazement to me that a small stretch of Tib Street has managed to hang on, just as it was.

That day we saw some finches in a pet shop, tiny, snuff-coloured birds with vivid red beaks and eye patches. They were delightful, we had to have some . . . But where would we keep them?

That was easy. In our bedroom there was a recess formed by the chimney breast; I made a large cage for them there by putting a front across it and perches and all the necessary things inside. This was fine, at first. We'd bought the finches in the autumn and the evenings were still light by the time we went up to bed. Then the clock went back for winter and the shorter day drew to a close and the finches settled themselves down the way birds will when darkness draws in. Later, we went upstairs to get ready for bed and put the light on . . .

Twitterings, hoppings, flutterings, as the tiny birds shook themselves awake, thinking it was daylight.

'They'll settle down,' I said, 'when we put the light out.'

But they didn't. I hadn't taken account of the effect of the sudden plunge into darkness when an electric light is switched off. The noise of several finches falling about all over the place has to be heard to be believed. 'They're *confused*,' Pat hissed at me.

'Confused?'

18

'Well of course. So would you be if you were only a bird and someone suddenly put the sun out.'

Fortunately for the finches – and for us – it wasn't long before the house next door became vacant and we moved into that. As soon as we moved, and had our own space around us – I began to fill it with birds. We were both out at work all day so it seemed only fair that Pat's budgie should be provided with a mate to keep it company. In the nature of things, two budgies became several, and after a while they were joined by other varieties: parakeets, cockateels, as well as the finches – who could get a decent night's sleep at last.

All these needed accommodation, and living amongst a clutter of cages standing about or sticking out from the walls was hardly practical, or comfortable; so wherever there was a recess, a likely corner, an alcove – I put a cage front across it. When the furniture could no longer be moved anywhere to make room for more, I made a small aviary in the spare bedroom. But the birds multiplied and the space went on shrinking. Still, we had our own yard now, there was nothing to stop us moving out into that and I could do what I'd always wanted: build an outdoor aviary.

It wasn't very large because there wasn't a great deal of room, a fair amount of the yard being taken up by an old brick-built air raid shelter, a relic of the war years that had lingered the way relics do. As I made my aviary I eyed that shelter . . . It could hardly be called functional any more, it certainly wasn't decorative and I couldn't see any museum making us an offer for it . . . No, the days of that shelter were definitely numbered.

In an area where the houses are crowded in on one another and everyone inevitably knows everyone else's business, it wasn't long before Pat and I came to be called 'the bird people'. Anyone who was interested, who wanted to look, to talk, to ask advice, came along to see us. Eventually, people began to turn up with their problems, too:

'Can you do anything with this?'

– It could have been a sparrow, a blackbird, a pigeon – just an injured bird handed over by someone I'd probably never seen before and, all too frequently, never saw again. I had the practical knowledge, the conscience that prompted me to do something, and the space; I was a natural dumping ground. It was fortunate that Pat's interest equalled mine, as she had to do most of the considerable cleaning our own birds and the strays caused, and a fair share of her housekeeping money went on their food.

Medicines were needed, too, and we began to get together a first-aid outfit. This was a necessity in more ways than one, as constant visits to the vet would have been far beyond our means and all too often the vet's verdict would be, 'Put it to sleep' – a piece of professional advice that nevertheless needed paying for. The few books I'd managed to get together as a source of pleasure as well as information were gradually being added to. I never turned anything down, and neither did Pat, we were always on the lookout in second-hand bookshops, jumbles and market stalls. Bit by bit we built up a library, modest, but comprehensive, ranging from seventeenth century treatises on hawking to reference books on the diseases of birds.

With people continuing to bring birds to us it was almost a matter of course that eventually we made contact with various animal aid societies and charities. At first our assistance was sought occasionally, then more and more frequently, until eventually official as well as voluntary societies, the police and private individuals referred to us whenever it was thought we could help.

It happened gradually, and over the years the contacts and birds accumulated. It was true that once there had been a first time, a stranger who knocked on the door and, standing in the dimness of the tiny porch, asked, 'Are you the bird people? Can you help?' But neither of us can remember that first time, it was too long ago, and too many birds have passed in and out of our house, occupying our lives sometimes briefly, sometimes for year after year. Many of them we have forgotten altogether, others we can never forget; but somewhere right at the beginning was one of the most memorable and beloved, the first kestrel to come into our kitchen. His name was Kit.

Two

Kit

Kit, who turned out to have the nature of a renegade and all the charm of a confidence trickster, was picked up one day unconscious and starving. The fact that he was wearing jesses proved that someone had tried to train him, but his wild nature and poor condition also proved that he had been badly handled and had escaped – or simply been given up for hopeless and turned loose.

Roaming free, weakened and confused, he had seen a budgie in a cage in the window of a house; driven by hunger and the instinct to swoop on his prey he had hurtled down and dashed himself against the glass. It was a terrible shock to the people in the house. They went out and looked beneath the window and found this dazed bird which they couldn't identify. They picked him up carefully, put him under an upturned washing basket and called the RSPCA to ask what they should do.

The branch they called was overworked and understaffed, fortunately, though, I'd had contact with them on previous occasions and they knew I was a responsible person with plenty of practical, general experience and as they already had too much on their hands it seemed the ideal solution to pass the bird on to me.

So when the RSPCA telephoned and asked if I would go along and have a look at a kestrel, see what could be done and possibly take charge of it, it never occurred to me to refuse. I simply asked directions and went. By the time I got there the bird was almost dead. During the time they had been keeping him the people who had found him – in an utterly well-meant but misguided attempt to do the right thing – had been feeding him seed, which was useless to a bird of prey.

I took him home and the first thing I did when I got there was feed him. By that time, from the number of birds we had taken in, Pat and I had learnt the importance of food – the absolute priority. In ninety-nine cases out of a hundred an injured bird meant a hungry bird. While we were looking to see what the damage was, what could be done, it could die of starvation with – well, not exactly plenty all around it, but at least always enough to keep it going. So no matter what state it was in, the first thing we did when we got hold of a bird was feed it. This had come to be a principle so basic it could be expressed in a few simple words: 'Feed them first, then get them right'.

Holding the soft-feathered, almost weightless body in my hand I offered small chunks of meat on my fingers. Kit's swift little head darted, his beak opened and snatched, hunger took second place to the indignity and strangeness of being grasped by a human being. If he sometimes got my finger by mistake, neither of us minded.

With food inside him it was not long before Kit recovered from his shocked state, although his physical condition, when I came to examine it, was bad. One side of the long, curved beak had a vertical split which made the beak grow sideways. He was very dirty, patches of his feathers were singed, as if they had deliberately been burned off, and a series of scabs had formed, spreading round his neck and down his chest.

After I had cleaned him up and treated him with ointment I put him out to live in the aviary in the yard. The other birds that at that time I still kept and bred were there – the parakeets, the love-birds, the zebra finches and cockateels, and Kit could not, of course, be let loose amongst them. Fortunately, the aviary was large enough to be partitioned. From his own section Kit eyed his exotic neighbours with interest and, supplementing the diet of raw meat on which I fed him, hunted the mice who found their way into his territory.

In time the scabs that had disfigured him came away and his new feathers grew. From the pathetic state of being what I could only describe as one hell of a mess he emerged as a neat little bird, his eyes bright, his smokey blue head and tawny, brown-flecked body shining and vital. He was always something of a weed, never attaining the full weight of a male kestrel – a tiercel – and a permanent let-down to his appearance, and inevitably his performance, were his broken tail feathers. Starvation had left its legacy in hunger traces, or hunger streaks.

In order to produce strong, healthy plumage a bird must be well fed from the fledgeling stage because the shaft (this is the long 'spine' that carries the thousands of interlocking barbs that make up the flight feather) of each growing feather is built up from the point where it emerges from the body. If a young bird has gone short of food the shafts are consequently undernourished and as they grow the effect is shown in the markings that are called hunger traces, weaknesses that make the feathers so brittle they can break off altogether; with each successive moult and new growth in the adult bird these traces reappear.

Fortunately, they can be mended by a method called imping. I took a short, triangular shaped imping needle and inserted it into a pigeon feather that had been trimmed to the appropriate length. The pigeon feather, by means of the exposed end of the imping needle, was then in its turn inserted into the existing stub of the bird's broken tail feather.

With these substitute feathers Kit had perfect flight; however, had he been turned loose the imped-in feather would have been thrown out in the spring when he moulted and the new feather broken off at its hunger trace as it grew. For balance and manoeuvrability his tail was vital to him in hunting. He might have been able to survive, although not very well, being unable to stoop on small, darting prey and having to rely on any beetles and insects he might be able to catch.

His beak, too, was no use to him in its damaged state. The deep split in it made it like a broken hinge – one or two hunting sorties and it would have snapped off entirely, leaving him totally unable to feed. I cut the beak as short as possible and for a long time kept it pared down; eventually, as the beak grew the split grew out with it.

His well-being assured, Kit grew fit and rather cheeky and was soon hopping so readily from his perch on to my fist that I

23

decided to train him.

Close by the house was a disused clay pit. A hundred feet deep, steep-sided, in places water had formed into lakes out of which, here and there, the ground rose in small islands. No one went there very much, it was isolated and quiet, out of the way of people and the noise of the traffic that thundered along to the nearby arterial roads. Shut in by the town I had no immediate access to the wind-swept open spaces romantically associated with hawking; but I had the clay pit, and that would do.

The training of a kestrel takes more than patience and knowledge. There is a curious, indefinable area where the identities of man and bird merge together, where each discovers the other's strengths and weaknesses, where the instincts of the bird are matched against the will of the man, and it is only by recognising these instincts and respecting the will of the bird that the man can succeed.

Someone, at some time, had tried to train Kit and failed. I was new to the game, to Kit it was only too familiar, there were associative memories of distress and confusion I could only guess at. I had gone a long way to winning the bird's trust; but if I made a slip I would get no second chance and Kit, once free, would be a speck in the sky, heading for the precarious freedom that was to him so much safer than the world of human beings.

There was one thing I established before I even took Kit out, and that was his fear of the hood. Hawking manuals insist that a falcon should be hooded between flights and when carried on the fist. There are a variety of reasons for this but Kit could hardly be expected to appreciate their finer points because he'd never read the hawking manuals, and the mere sight of the hood caused him distress. The instinctive communication that by then existed between us enabled me to understand that this was not temperament, or cussedness, but fear. To stick blindly to the rules would mean the imposition of sheer human force – I suspected this had happened to Kit too often, too roughly, and I could not see a workable relationship progressing from any repetition of it. I decided to rely on my commonsense, and as things turned out I was right.

24

Kit knew me and trusted me, he knew my voice. I tied a creance – which is a long leash – on to Kit's jesses, put on an old motoring glove, took Kit on my fist and stepped out of the front door. And I talked. All the way down the road to the clay pit, I talked. Oblivious of my surroundings or of the effect I was having on the neighbours, I talked. Kit, obviously intrigued and just a little wary, took occasional glances at the world about him, then his attention returned to the reassurance of my familiar voice. His small head tilted this way and that, his bright eyes regarded me with interest, his claws gripped the glove possessively – in a sense, I was his territory, and as his territory turned out to be mobile, he would go with it wherever it went.

Another traditional necessity I dispensed with were the bells for Kit's legs. These are tiny bells attached to a soft leather thong called a bewit, and they are an aid to the falconer in locating a bird when it is flying free. If, for instance, it landed in a tree, it would be thoroughly camouflaged in a matter of seconds; the slightest movement, however, and the bells would tinkle, pinpointing its whereabouts.

Kit was strong and fast but exceptionally small, and so light it seemed scarcely possible he could take off encumbered by any extra weight. And another very important factor I had to take into account was my own inexperience. There was an even chance that when I dispensed with the creance I would lose Kit; an under-weight kestrel with a split beak and unreliable tail feathers would have a tough enough fight for survival without the additional handicap of a bell on each leg.

In the clay pit Kit was soon flying on the creance, answering my whistle. Very soon Pat joined me in his training – or, I should say, our training, because all three of us were learning all the time. With Kit still on the creance, Pat would take him on her glove and carry him away, a distance of about twenty yards; I whistled, she cast him off, he flew to me and I gave him a small piece of meat as a reward. Pat came to collect him – and so the procedure was repeated. Gradually, we widened the distance until he was flying about sixty yards. Then we took to changing about, with me carrying Kit and Pat taking the creance, calling him with a whistle so he flew from me to her and she rewarded him.

Then, for the first nerve-wracking time, I untied the creance from the jesses.

Pat walked away with Kit on her glove, talking to him just as I did. He was just as much at home with her, and having craftily sorted out the game in his little head often went through the tactic of trying to peer round her to see where I was standing with the little piece of meat that was his reward. She scolded him for being so cheeky; then she halted, turned, and cast him off.

He soared up, flying free, hovering. I waited; he seemed to be a very long way away. In those few moments I wondered if this was the last I'd ever see of my bird. Then Kit spotted me, and made straight for me. The joy, the relief, the sense of achievement I felt when my first kestrel, flying free, landed on my fist for the first time will always give a lift to my heart. My pride was equally divided – in myself for having won his trust, in him for being such a clever little bird.

Next, I made a lure. This is a small pad with pigeon's wings attached – in effect, a dummy bird. I would put the meat on the lure and hold the lure up for Kit to fly to; having to take the meat this way he became accustomed to the lure and interested in it.

I fixed a length of twine to the lure and we progressed to the next stage. Kit, cast off by Pat, soared, circled, choosing his moment to streak swift as an arrow on to the lure as I swung it round and round. As encouragement, I always let him take the lure the first time, then I would whip it away and hide it. Kit would swoop up into the air and plane about, searching keenly for the prey that had so unaccountably vanished; as soon as I edged it into sight again he made for it as hard as he could.

All this time Kit was flying free. I had decided that once the creance was off it was off for good, there were to be no second thoughts or attacks of uncertainty, even when Kit was at his most maddening and uncooperative. Because I had come to know him. I knew when he was feeling wilful, or out of sorts, when he was just plain moody and out to stretch my patience to the limit, or when he was in the mind to amuse himself by playing tricks.

He sheered away once, in the early days, careering about the sky and showing off. Pat stayed at the bottom of the clay pit and called, I laboriously climbed to the top and tried from there. My success was almost immediate. Kit seemed to whip out of nowhere and began stooping enthusiastically again and again to the lure. I noticed Pat waving, signalling, jumping up and down, calling, but her voice was lost across the distance. I couldn't understand what had set her off and thought she might perhaps be congratulating me in a rather overexcited way; although something about her gestures indicated exasperation.

Puzzled, I tried to follow the direction in which she was pointing; I was still swinging the lure and Kit was still taking it. Then I saw . . . it was not *my* bird at all, it was another one.

I looked frantically around. A pair of bright eyes regarded me from ground level . . . Kit had sneaked back on the scene and was standing close by, studying with interest the antics of his incomprehensible human being and wild kestrel.

For a change of scenery one day we took Kit to a nearby park. He enjoyed the car – he had a bossy way of deciding when something or someone belonged to him: Pat and I were his; at the clay pit he had his own special mound for a dust bath and would never go anywhere else; the rear shelf of the car was his and he paraded up and down, peering out of the window.

He emerged from the car in a lordly manner, surveyed the park, flew straight into a tree and stayed there. Recognising one of Kit's moods, I settled down to wait.

I waited four hours. I wouldn't give in, neither would Kit; sooner or later one of us had to win. Pat went home for a flask of coffee. Dusk began to close in.

An elderly gentleman and a little girl, walking by, paused to watch. The girl asked me what I was doing.

'I'm calling my bird,' I answered carefully, with some distant doubts about my patience and my voice holding out.

Children are natural mimics. The little girl searched in the grass, found a worm and held it up exactly as I was holding up the lure, calling 'Here, birdie.' It made sense to her. It made sense to Kit, too – he flew straight down on to her small hand.

But telegraph wires were his favourite. He seemed to enjoy the sense of being extremely conspicuous and totally out of reach. One day he sat himself up in some and refused to come down, haughtily ignoring me. A small group of children watched fascinated as I held up pieces of meat, whistled, called, walked about. It went on for such a long time that one small boy, impelled by the desire to do something helpful, came up to me – I had no attention to spare for anyone except Kit – tugged at my coat and said earnestly, 'Mister . . . I think your bird's deaf.'

Pat walking in front of her home, numbers 37 and 39

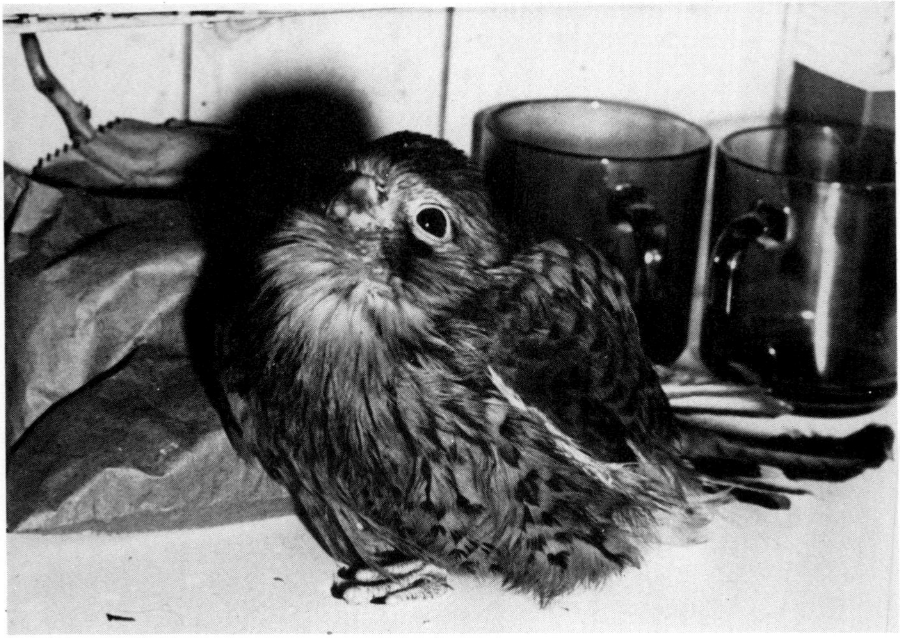

(*above*) A female kestrel.(*below*) Charles, a twenty-two year old crow with a stolen
piece of cheese. Unable to fly he goes everywhere fearlessly on foot

Wol the owl (*above*) standing on the nursery stairs and (*below*) coming down with Tich the black cat

The livingroom (*above*) Pat is sewing, Bob is watching the racing results while Tich and Clara the hen share the top of the TV set and Baby the goose wanders about. (*below*) Pat is reading with her cat Dinah on her lap and Jeannie a South American Fishing Hawk looks over her shoulder

Three

Owls

We hadn't had Kit very long when one evening the phone rang. A voice, completely strange to me, enquired, 'Are you the bird man?'

I said I was.

'Then you're now the owner of a little owl,' the voice continued.

'Am I? All right,' I said philosophically. 'But just as a matter of interest, would you mind telling me why?'

The facts were that two people had been out driving in the country and seen a bird hit by a car. They stopped, got out and went to have a look to see if they could do anything. They discovered it was an owl, still alive; not prepared to leave him there at the side of the road they took him home and sought out a nearby vet who treated his injuries. Having accomplished this kindness they were uncertain what to do next. They could not keep the owl at home and they could scarcely take him back and put him down where they had found him as he was still too injured to look after himself.

The vet, in the course of his profession, was regularly in touch with people and societies that had to do with helping animals and somewhere, in association with these, he had heard something about us. He didn't know my name, or where I lived, but because somebody had to do something, he made enquiries here and there and eventually came up with our telephone number.

So, by this random route, the little owl (who was christened Hootie) arrived. The latin name of this type of owl is *Athena noctua* but it is known as the little owl because that is precisely what it is, the smallest of our English owls; it flies by day as well as night and generally does its hunting at dusk and dawn.

Eight and a half inches high, injured, wary, but never for a moment losing his confidence, he perched on the back of a chair in the kitchen, glaring out of his beautiful yellow eyes. His beak was razor sharp, no movement of it was discernible but strange clacking sounds came from it.

'What's that noise?' Pat asked cautiously.

'He's warning me off,' I said – which might have seemed ridiculous on a comparison of the owl's size and my thirteen stone but it was nevertheless true.

Hootie ate readily enough, which was just as well because the medicine that had been prescribed by the vet could be given in the form of drops and powder on his food. When he had eaten he was left for a while to take account of his new surroundings. Later, clacking indignantly, he allowed himself to be handled by me and carried upstairs.

The aviary in the spare bedroom was empty, having lately been vacated by two peach-faced love-birds who were supposed to breed but had preferred to spend their time chewing through the ceiling into the attic. They'd made a terrible mess in the process, but the hole had been repaired and the aviary was ready for use again. I put Hootie in there for a period of convalescence, so that I could keep an eye on him and watch how his injuries were healing.

All that weekend I attended to the little owl, but on Monday I had to go off to work. I'd been at Wynstay House for several years and while Pat had stayed on there I'd gone to another firm, moving from instrument making to tool making. I was doing shift work then and while I was out it was Pat's turn to take over with Hootie.

In spite of their diminutive size little owls are reputed to be fierce and have been known to tackle hen-pheasants. Pat was not a hen-pheasant, she was a fully grown human being who, nevertheless found herself in the faintly surrealistic situation of being menaced by a very small bird.

As she stepped into the aviary Hootie performed a rapid

sideways movement along his perch to put himself in a position where he could glare straight down into her face. He drew himself up to his impressive eight and a half inches and clacked non-stop. Pat looked at the razor beak and vice-like talons and thought: he's going to jump on my head . . .

She dismissed this thought as unworthy of her habitual commonsense and, anyway, what would it matter if he did? It wouldn't kill her, and it wasn't as if she'd just had an expensive hair-do or was even unaccustomed to being used as a perch, in a household perpetually full of birds the odd one sitting on her head occasionally could be looked on as an occupational commonplace.

Wondering what telepathic means one employed to reassure an angry owl, she resorted to rational, positive thinking: you don't *know* I'm going to be nice to you. You don't *know* I'm only here to feed you. But I am. So there . . .

She put the bowl of food near him and retired firmly. As she watched from outside the aviary Hootie subsided in a rather nonplussed way, stopped clacking, and made for his food. 'There. See?' Pat said, but he ignored her.

After very little time his aggression turned to caution, then by degrees to friendliness. He had suffered a smashed wing as a result of the accident and was never able to fly again. When eventually he went to the outdoor aviary his method of propulsion was somewhere between a flutter and a curious, toddling walk.

He settled down without any fuss and soon discovered that when he came from under cover out to the open part of aviary he was in sight of the kitchen window. There was a rose tree in a tub in that part of the aviary; he would perch on the side of it and wait, staring at the window with his brilliant eyes until someone in the house caught sight of him. Whoever came to the window – Pat or myself – would nod at him; he'd give an answering nod, hop down from the tub and toddle under cover again.

For the rest of his life he did that, choosing his own time. We never knew how long he perched there, sometimes in the pouring rain we would look out and see a drenched, persistent owl, huddled into himself, staring patiently. Then one day he didn't come out. When I went to look for him – half knowing that the food I took was no longer needed – I found that the little owl had died in the night.

Death was something we knew we had to accept. We cared, our caring has always been expressed in practical and unsentimental way; when Pat sheds tears over a bird it's generally when she's busy getting the ointment out or the food ready for the next one.

That was the case when Hootie died. By then we had another owl, a tawny that had come to us through the RSPCA. This was another case where the combination of kindness and ignorance almost resulted in death by starvation: the people who had found him, not knowing that raw meat is the essential diet of a bird of prey, had been trying to feed him on boiled ham and peas.

Once again, my first job on getting the owl home was to feed him. I perched him on the back of a chair in the kitchen and put a large raw chicken leg beside him, then I turned away for a moment to say something to Pat. The owl suddenly launched himself off the chair and fluttered up on to the pelmet over the window.

'He's dropped his food,' Pat said, and together we hunted around the floor and the cushions of the chair. Then we realised the owl hadn't dropped it, he had been so famished he hadn't attempted to hold the meat in his claw and rip at it – he'd swallowed it whole.

We called him Barney. He was already half tame and plainly the victim of a cruelly amateur attempt at wing clipping – a measure undertaken to prevent birds from flying away.

The end of a bird's wings are constructed of a series of small bones – the phalanges, the metacarpus and the carpi; from the base of the carpi another phalange projects at an angle. All this follows the rudimentary pattern of human bone structure, corresponding to fingers, hand, wrist. The thicker of the phalanges, at the base of the carpi, carries the bird's flight feathers and if the barbs of these feathers are clipped the bird is not then

32

capable of flight. The barbs don't grow again, the shaft works its way out during the next moulting process and is replaced by a new feather; when moulting is finished the bird is once again airborne.

That's the theory, the practice, obviously, has to be performed with care. The job on Barney had been done clumsily and in ignorance; the entire section of delicate, interlocking bones had been hacked off – in human terms this would be the equivalent to the amputation of a hand.

Owls need somewhere to live. They make a terrible mess of a house if they're kept in all the time, and they need a constant diet of raw meat, which is either expensive to buy or extremely troublesome to come by. Having acquired Barney, permanently crippled him, then found him too costly and too much of a nuisance to keep, the one-time owner had turned him out to fend for himself.

This was something he could not do. His wing had already healed and after his first moult the feathers grew beyond their normal length – that being nature's way of compensating him by balancing him out, but he had lost the agile and stealthy flight that would enable him to hunt. He flew lop-sidedly, making loud whirring sounds, signalling his approach with a noise like a helicopter. For Barney there could nevermore be unsuspecting prey, the mice and voles that were his diet would hear him long before he arrived; handicapped as he was he would soon starve.

So Barney, being dependent on human beings to feed him, had come to stay. He divided his time between the outdoor aviary and the house and was soon completely tame.

In the house the stairs go up directly from the kitchen and the area beneath them I'd turned into a large cage. Between the end of the cage and the door that lets into the hall is a square recess. To bridge the space across this recess I put up a strong wooden bar to act as a perch. This was one of Barney's favourite places from which he could look at things in the kitchen or watch the two mynah birds in the cage beneath the stairs. He had the gravity common to his species and in addition to that an extremely dignified, long-suffering air, like a rather fussy uncle set in his ways. His special treat was the gravy from tinned dog food, Pat patiently held a spoon full of it for him while he slurped it up with terrible noises and great relish.

Like Kit, he would go anywhere with us and took happily to the car, sharing the back shelf with Kit. For minute after minute they would perch side by side, staring unblinkingly, absolutely immobile, like two stuffed birds. Then, in response to their own whim, they'd change places, shuffling round each other and freezing again into total stillness. Or they would take a walk, backwards and forwards, crossing and recrossing with clockwork precision, as if someone had wound them up. It became a regular thing for fascinated motorists to follow our car for miles, watching the antics of the birds.

Barney's favourite method of travel was under Pat's coat. He would creep inside, making small movements of his downy body until he was quite comfortable. He half clung to her, she half carried him; sooner or later a gently measured snoring indicated he had dropped off to sleep. If she stopped to speak to anyone he would wake up, listen for a moment, then struggle out to see what was going on.

Pat grew so accustomed to carrying an inquisitive owl about with her that she ceased to think of how he would appear to strangers. One day when she was outside the supermarket talking to a friend a short-sighted dog lover, catching sight of the small face peering out from Pat's coat, descended in a great rush of affection, crying, 'A Pekinese, a dear little Pekinese, I must stroke it –' and before Pat could say anything she had tried to. It was such a shock to her to encounter a beak she fled in confusion.

Baby owls that had been abandoned by their mothers, crawled too soon from their nests – or been taken from them by boys – these came at the appropriate time of the year to us, via the RSPCA.

They didn't come in ones and twos, they came in groups, boxes full of tiny bundles of down, jostling and squeaking to be fed, so small they had to have meat pushed into their beaks – and this had to be done every two hours. It was an exhausting

34

business, every two hours meant exactly that, round the clock, not just when it was conveniently daylight.

By then Pat had given up her job. After her mother's death her father's health, never very good, deteriorated even more and he became an invalid, so she had to be at home to be able to look after him, which she was able to do as he continued to live next door to us.

She still prepared slides for the laboratory, being able to do this at home, using the front room to work in. That meant she was always about to see to the birds, but the baby owls still put a considerable strain on her – on us both, in fact. During the night we kept the boxes of youngsters beside our bed and took it in turns to roll out and feed them when the alarm rang. By the morning, bleary-eyed and scarcely on speaking terms, we had lost count of the number of times we'd got up, and very often we never even knew when we'd taken each other's turn by mistake.

There was also the possibility – as the owls tended to crowd together and all looked alike, anyway – that the strongest and greediest were getting food intended for their neighbours. In the daytime this problem was solved with the help of Barney. Pat had the food cut up and ready, the youngsters were lined up and Barney plonked amongst them. The presence of an adult bird triggered off a response: the tiny heads tilted, the tiny beaks gaped; Pat rushed along the line, shoving in food, making sure each got his share, no more and no less.

One charming creature, so small it could fit into a breakfast cup, had ventured out of its nest too early, rolled down a roof and fallen into a gutter. Someone had seen this happen but not thought to report it to the RSPCA for two days. During that time the baby owl lay helpless, ignored by the mother owl who flew over him with food for her other youngsters. It must have been sheer chance that she had stuffed this one so full he had enough to sustain him; if there had been any rain the gutter would have flooded and he'd have drowned; a cold wind would have finished him off, but the weather was warm and dry. By this combination of favourable circumstances he survived to take his place with the others, squeaking faintly and ravenous.

In spite of the incessant eek-eek-eek that punctuated our lives for weeks, in spite of the lack of sleep and sheer physical drag of cutting up food and getting it into the right beak, we found the small owls completely endearing. Countless comical creatures all over the place, fluffy and round-eyed, asked to be picked up, stroked and cuddled. But the temptation had to be resisted, for the sake of the birds themselves. They had to be returned to their natural environment as soon as possible. The longer they were kept away, the more they were handled, the less chance they had to adapt and survive when they were turned out to look after themselves.

There have been many times when I've been asked by the police to go and catch a bird – a magpie or an owl – that people complain has been flying at them and attacking them. In nine cases out of ten I could guarantee that the bird had been taken very young from its nest and reared as a pet. Under the Protection of Birds Act, which I shall go into later, this is in fact an offence, but people still do it. A bird treated in this way never learns – by necessity, imitation or the development of instinct – what its function is. Never knowing anything except human beings it becomes humanised itself and once turned loose goes up to people, expecting them to look after it, because that is all it understands.

On one occasion I was called out to attend to a tawny owl that had been reported to the police as 'bothering people'. Indignantly beaten off many times it had eventually taken itself away to sit motionless in a poplar tree for two days and nights.

When I shinned up the tree the owl came to me straight away, with pathetic friendliness, eager for the food I had taken along in my pocket. Round one leg it wore what I at first sight took to be a jess. On inspection, this turned out to be a do-it-yourself kind of tether, adapted from a piece of dog collar – a sure sign the owl had been kept by someone as a pet. Whatever had happened – whether it had found its way outdoors one day and wandered off, or whether it had been turned loose because it was too much trouble to keep – one thing was certain: with no idea how to look for its own food it had simply been sitting waiting in the tree for someone to come along and feed it.

I took him home and kept him in the house for a while. There he took his place with the other birds, learning gradually – and with a great deal of bickering – that if he didn't grab his food and hold on to it, someone would pinch it off him. Then he went to the aviary, where he had a chance of growing steadily less tame; but he still remained stubbornly attached to human beings, flying down when anyone approached and standing by the wire, squeaking for attention.

The baby owls progressed in their feeding, taking more each meal so they could go for longer intervals until eventually they were able to feed themselves. As soon as that happened they went outdoors and were never handled at all.

I'd gradually given up cage birds as more and more of our space was taken up with strays. The aviary I'd made in the yard just wasn't big enough, so down came that old air raid shelter and on to the space I'd gained I built a much bigger aviary. In there the baby owls stayed about a month, in surroundings as close to natural as possible, slowly adapting from the diurnal pattern imposed on them to their normal nocturnal habits. Then, when there was a spell of mild weather, it was time for them to go.

The night before they were released they were not fed; unless they had caught any of the mice that venture into the aviary they went hungry. In the morning, we put them into boxes and drove out to wooded country. There, we took the owls from the boxes and cast them up into the trees. Some owls fluttered up for themselves, some had to be sat on branches; all of them, because they were hungry, would sooner or later start searching for food, taking insects and worms at first until they learned to hunt properly.

To make sure everything was all right we revisited the wood over the next few days. Wherever possible, we like to choose an area where we know someone, someone who would keep an eye on things and report if there was an owl around who wasn't behaving as it should. As far as we know there has never been a failure. The months of care and expense might never have happened, the owls have learned to fend for themselves, they have paired off and flown away . . . Which, we console ourselves each time we trudge back through the woods to our waiting car, is what it's all about, anyway.

Four

The turkey thing

Kit had become a fine hunter, his prey starlings and sparrows. He killed them instantly, with the grip of his talons; I took them from him, rewarded him with his share and kept the rest for the common larder. But no matter how many Kit caught he could not keep up with the demands of the birds which were now filling our house. Friends who went out on shooting parties brought back hares, rabbits and pigeons; farmers I'd got to know rang up occasionally to offer a sheep that had been knocked over by a motorist or savaged and killed by a dog.

I never refused anything, I couldn't afford to. I went out regularly myself to shoot, but I wanted another working bird. I was keen to extend my practical knowledge of hawking – and whatever it caught, the bird would feed not only itself but a few of the others, too.

It was while I was turning this over in my head that I saw a buzzard advertised for sale in the local paper. I'd read a lot about buzzards but I'd never owned one, I wasn't sure what to do. I looked at the address and saw it wasn't all that far from us. 'Let's just go and look at it,' I suggested to Pat. And as proof I wasn't going out with the deliberate intention of buying I didn't take any money with me.

Pat knew better. She knew 'Let's just look,' really meant 'Let's go and get it'. So she took the housekeeping along in her purse, which was just as well, because before the end of the evening I'd borrowed it off her.

Buzzards have a reputation for docility and cowardice, they are also said to be lazy – characteristics that hardly show buzzards up in a good light but make them good beginner's birds.

This one was overweight and had a vile temper, but I didn't hesitate. I saw a confused and aggressive bird kept in miserable conditions and I bought her. If I could do nothing with her I would simply release her, anything rather than leave her where she was.

Unavoidably, the journey back caused further confusion for the buzzard. She had to be put in a cardboard box and taken first to a friend of ours to be weighed – this was important because a hawk, to be brought to good flying order, must be the correct weight – at home we had no adequate scales of our own.

When we arrived at our friend's house the buzzard was released from the box and as soon as she was out she went for me, slashing at me with her vicious talons, fastening on with a savagery that drew blood. We jessed her while she clung to me and somehow managed to weigh her. She had been fed on tins of dog food and the occasional rat that had been caught in a trap; she was much too heavy but in spite of that in fairly good condition, although a few of her flight feathers were broken.

After she had been weighed we had to go through the upheaval of getting her in the car again to take her home. I didn't want to increase her distress by putting her in the box again, so I gave Pat a glove to wear and told her to sit in the passenger seat. Then I picked up the furious, flapping bird and shoved her on Pat's fist. 'Hang on. Don't let her fly off –'

Face to face, Pat and the buzzard stared it out while I raced round the car and flung myself into the driving seat. I said, 'She's too heavy. We'll get her weight down and bring her back at the end of the week to weigh her again.'

'We won't,' Pat said. 'I'm not going through this performance again. We buy your own damn scales.'

That night the buzzard, who was called Perdita, was put in the back bedroom, using for her perch a cast-iron stand that had once held an old-fashioned wringer. About every hour I'd get up and go and have a look at her; as she was causing the maximum disturbance, anyway, I didn't have much choice.

She pulled the iron stand over with a tremendous crash and somehow managed to drag it halfway across the room. I wondered whether to put it upright but decided if I did she'd only pull it over again and the entire night would go by in noise and struggling and everyone getting more and more bad-tempered. Eventually she quietened down and we all managed to get some sleep.

The next morning I put up a screen perch – a bar nailed across two joists with a sack over the bar. She sat there all day, too enraged and upset to eat, every time I went near her she slashed out at me. I knew that in the mood she was in, and with claws so strong and sharp, she had the power to open up a tin, just like a tin opener. I dared not think what sort of damage she would do, had she got hold of me, but still I stayed near her, trying to coax her to eat. I spent all Saturday and Sunday sitting with her, talking to her, and at last – on the Sunday evening, she took a piece of meat from me.

By doing this she acknowledged me as a provider of food and established the connection between food and the glove. This did not, initially, do anything to improve her temper; I'd offer her food on the glove, she'd knock the glove about in an absolute fury, then she'd take the food. As her diet was restricted she had less bulk to put into her attacks; rapidly thinning down she grew grudgingly cooperative, and after much patient trial and error I got her to step from the perch to the glove.

As Perdita was totally untrained I wanted to make a start flying her as soon as possible, but it was the middle of winter and too dark for me to take her out by the time I got home from work. I decided that the only way was to begin at home, flying her across the kitchen; to do this I first had to carry her downstairs.

She was getting on to my fist readily enough by then, but the stairs were a different matter. I carried her across the room and out on to the small landing; distrustful of every move she sat on my fist, seething. The stairs were steep and narrow and closed in; halfway down she'd had enough – she bated wildly, thrashing her wings and hurling herself off my fist.

I wasn't going back. If Perdita wasn't battling at me with her claws she was doing it with her will, and if I once started the habit of giving in to her, she'd know it, and in the end I'd lose completely. So I carried on, holding her by her jesses just as she

41

was and emerged in the kitchen with her hanging upside down from my fist, for all the world like a great, daft pear.

Day after day she repeated this performance, always choosing the halfway point. Then she suddenly changed tactics and bated as soon as I got out of the bedroom and to the top of the stairs. It made no difference, she had to learn that where I went she went, she could do it in any manner she liked but that was the limit of her choice; sooner or later she had to do it my way.

But time after time I carried her, suspended by her jesses, all the way down the stairs. I was careful to see she never knocked herself and I was never rough with her; I just went on being slightly more bloody-minded than she was and in the end she gave in. One evening she sat quietly on my fist all the way and after that never gave any more trouble coming downstairs.

Pat was accustomed to all kinds of birds: pathetic creatures that aroused her protectiveness, comical ones that appealed to her sense of humour, independent ones that commanded her respect, but Perdita was a bird all on her own and Pat didn't know quite what attitude to take with her. There was no positive response, much less a rapport – 'I can't seem to think of her as a bird, as such,' Pat said. 'More of a sort of turkey thing.'

She was being insulting, deliberately. 'Don't call her that,' I said.

'She doesn't know,' Pat countered, reasonably enough.

'Well, *I* do,' I said. I was protective of my bird's dignity, although Perdita – sulking, screeching, hanging upside down and generally flinging herself about like a cartoon bird – didn't appear to give much thought to it herself.

In the kitchen Perdita learned to fly on a creance, that was something else to which she objected but I was beginning to think there was nothing in the world that could win her favour. Some evenings she'd cooperate, other evenings, although she was ravenously hungry, she would sit immovable, refusing to fly towards the food I held out for her.

I had to keep her on either a creance or a leash because by then we'd acquired two Siamese cats, Tan and Ming. Pat and I had always been cat lovers and we didn't see why having birds about the place should deprive us of cats as well. But we had a system: everything that came into the house, if it looked as if it was going to spend any time with us, even only a couple of days, was introduced to the cats. Or them to it. Cats are regal, possessive and inquisitive, they have to *know*, and particularly they have to be sure that our care and affection is fairly portioned out. As long as we're there it doesn't matter much what else is, so our cats, having been brought up with birds, regard everything with wings as a friend. If Pat was sitting down with Perdita on her fist, Tan would stroll casually under the chair and Ming would try to climb up on to Pat's lap to see what was going on. I had to dive to get them before Perdita did. Sometimes I wasn't quick enough; Perdita had several lumps out of Ming's bottom before Ming learned to keep clear of her.

When Perdita at last accepted me to the point of flying unhesitatingly to me, I knew it was time to take her outdoors – first of all to get her to eat away from the environment she had grown accustomed to, then to get her to fly to me.

It was still winter and in the dark nights the clay pit was out of the question, the best I could do was walk about the streets. Every evening I took her out, walking the narrow, lamplit, quiet streets, the deserted alleyways, coaxing her to eat in these unfamiliar, ever-changing surroundings.

She was distrustful, defensive, her attention everywhere, too disturbed sometimes to eat, although I walked with her for hours or simply stood on the corner, talking to her, the rain filling up my gumboots. It was almost a week before she was sufficiently confident outdoors to take food from the glove.

But at weekends I could take her to the clay pit. I flew her short lengths at first, from Pat to myself, gradually lengthening the distance, just as I had done with Kit. While she was still on the creance I took her out to wooded country and cast her up into a tree and called her to make sure she would fly down to me. I was learning, along with the bird. I found that if I put her in a tree and then went around kicking up the undergrowth, Perdita would pounce on anything that moved.

Once Perdita was flying over a distance of ten yards I was as certain of her as I would ever be and I took the creance off. She was mean tempered and unpredictable, but she was a working bird, and work she did. The partnership was essentially practical and I couldn't pretend there was any love lost between us; there was respect – grudging on Perdita's side, on mine completely sincere. To me every bird is a miracle of flesh and bone, muscle and feather, and Perdita – with her brooding poise, her soaring flight, her brilliant yellow eyes and sleek plumage – Perdita was beautiful, too.

And a sneak, and a termagant, squawking, glaring, sulking; swelling to twice her normal size to dive on the cats; sitting clamped to the branch of a tree, refusing to budge because she just didn't feel like working; indulging herself in violent, capricious hatreds: buses, pillarboxes, Labrador dogs . . . Just Labradors, other breeds she'd ignore, Labradors threw her into a frenzy. She hated the wet; if I dared to take her out in the rain she somehow managed to make herself go tall and thin with indignation. When I cast her off she made no attempt to fly but fell like a stone, landing with a thud on the ground and just sitting there, scowling up at me.

But Perdita worked. Craftily, tirelessly, with remarkable agility for so large a bird, displaying an intricate precision in barbed wire and tangled undergrowth, a breathtaking pounce from absolute immobility, a lightning-bolt drop from her lazy, soaring flight.

She made a mistake once, only once. I had taken her out to an abandoned aerodrome some miles away, a deserted place with acres of open ground and only the remains of buildings and Nissen huts. I put her up and she went after a rabbit, flying at her powerful maximum impetus and speed, so intent on her quarry that when the rabbit bolted into a Nissen hut she didn't see it in time. She crashed head on. She was flung upwards, badly shaken, and flapped dazedly about. I called her to my fist and she came straight away. I wanted to make sure she was all right. As far as I could tell all she had was a slightly cross-eyed look which I took to be the effect of the collision.

But there was more to it than that. Perdita was thinking. No rabbit ever got away from her by diving into a Nissen hut again.

As soon as it tried that tactic she remembered and whipped over the top of the hut and waited at the other side for it to come out.

From the beginning I made sure she understood she must surrender her prey to me. When she made a kill she would be on the ground with it, holding it in her claw ready to rip it and eat it. I went in to her steadily, without fuss, talking to her. As I slipped the leash through her jesses she gave me exactly the respectful attention I was giving her. I offered her the glove, her talons released the prey to me; she stepped on to my fist and took the reward I had ready for her.

In all our dealings there was this fine edged balance of understanding. Buzzards have long been held in low esteem, scorned for their lazy and allegedly cowardly characteristics, but recognising that Perdita is a bird on her own I've never underestimated her. Someone who was out hawking with me once made the mistake of treating her in the traditionally contemptuous manner, snatching her prey from her with the over-confident words, 'It's only a buzzard'. I wasn't surprised at her reaction – although he was; glove or no glove, she almost had his thumb off. He has revised his opinion since then.

Once I thought I'd lost her. It was when she was first flying free. Pat and I had taken her to some meadows where there were trees and a few farm buildings scattered about. As soon as I released her jesses she made off, using one of her short spurts of speed to get herself out of sight in no time.

I called . . . and we waited . . . Usually she wore a bell in her tail feathers but it was no good listening for that because this was one occasion I hadn't put it on her. When we tired of waiting and there was no sign of her, we began to search, backwards and forwards, then working away from each other in ever widening circles.

The time went by. I thought of the scruffy, fat turkey thing with her obscure dislikes and unpredictable tantrums who hated the rain and would have pounced on the cats if she'd got the chance. I thought of the proud, majestic, maddening creature she had become and I admit I was gloomily reconciling myself to having seen the last of her.

Pat, conscientiously trudging the fields and calling from time to time, was aware of herself being watched by two men working in the piggeries at the farm buildings. 'Lost your dog, missus?'

'Er – no. It's a hawk I've lost. A buzzard. You haven't seen one, have you?' she said, feeling a fool.

They said no, looking at her as if she was. 'But if we do, we'll let you know,' they added pityingly.

For over an hour we searched, returning to the area where Perdita had disappeared and searching again there until we were on the point of giving up. Then a movement in a tree caught my attention. It was Perdita. She had been playing her own version of hide-and-seek, sneaking back to the place where she had originally vanished. When I held up the glove she flew down and perched on it, staring at me with a half-angry composure that said plainly, 'You're not all that clever, are you?'

We did wonder, though, why she had taken it into her head to behave like that. Afterwards, it dawned on me that she had been expressing her resentment at a change in routine. She had always flown from Pat to me, it was the first time we'd tried to reverse the procedure. After that, we made sure she learned to fly to Pat.

She did it (as she does most things) with malevolence. Pat handles birds firmly and affectionately, not putting up with any nonsense, but under her commonsense exterior there is a great deal of gentleness. The sight of Perdita, flying straight at her, yellow eyes burning, beak open and squawking, made her tremble. She'd shut her eyes, stick her arm out and hope for the best.

She was accustomed to the charming and gallant Kit; a painful lesson brought home to her the difference in temperament between the two birds. One time Perdita flew to her – from me – and was perched on her glove. One of the jesses was in the correct place, dangling forward over the palm of Pat's hand and ready to be gathered up, but the other had trailed over the back.

Birds are never held by one jess; automatically Pat made to take up the trailing jess with her unprotected right hand. She didn't do it quickly enough, and perhaps she fumbled – she was never quite sure. Before she knew what had happened Perdita had snatched at her thumb, driving her hind claw in, right down, embedding it in the flesh. There was no question of shaking off a grip so relentless, or even, I found when I ran to help Pat, of prising it off; I had to rip the claw from the flesh. Pat's thumb swelled up like a balloon and for weeks afterwards she couldn't use it properly.

That wasn't the only time Perdita drew blood from her. There was the matter of the bath and – again – Perdita's lightningly unpredictable temper.

We had an improvised pond in the aviary in the yard, not a very good one but it had to do until I got around to making something better. It was all right for the smaller birds but wouldn't do for Perdita, since there was too little space both in it and around it. Directly opposite our house, across the narrow road, is a strip of green backed by a high wall which could be said to serve us as a front garden. At a quiet time of day we took a large bowl of water out there, and Perdita, pegged the end of her leash down and let her get on with it.

It wasn't in Perdita's nature to do anything without fuss. Even when she was enjoying herself she had to cause the maximum to-do, thrashing her wings and chucking water about until she'd almost emptied the bowl. Pat went into the house to get another bucket of water as a refill and returned to the grass with it. The minute she approached the bowl there was a blur of movement at ground level – Perdita, furiously reacting to the possibility that Pat was about to take her bath away, jumped sideways and sank her claws in Pat's leg.

It was all so quick Pat was scarcely aware of what had happened even as she was doing something about it. She dropped the bucket, looked down, saw her leg pouring with blood and Perdita clinging to it. She had no glove on but she didn't even think of that; purely as a reflex action she stooped and tugged at the leash. For once, Perdita released her hold straight away. She had made her point. Considerably put out, she returned to her bath while Pat limped indoors for first aid.

During one working day, while I was checking a machine, something went wrong with the mechanism and I emerged with a broken wrist. I had to wear a plaster cast and Perdita, running true to type, hated it from the word go. I couldn't think what to do. I couldn't get Pat to cart the buzzard about, but instead she came up with a solution – or thought she had. She went to a great deal of trouble to make a leather cover for my plaster cast, hoping that Perdita would accept it as a new and slightly different glove, but it didn't fool the buzzard. Rigid with outrage, she allowed herself to be plonked on my fist and carried to the clay pit; the minute I released her she made straight for an island in one of the lakes in the clay pit and sat there swearing at me.

It was on one of these lakes that she once went after a duck. Skimming over the water with her low, powerful flight, she snatched at the duck and missed, clouting it with her claws and sending up clouds of feathers. She landed on a railway sleeper that was floating nearby and had poised herself ready to pounce when suddenly the air was filled with a flock of gulls.

It seemed to me that everything happened in the blink of an eyelid. One minute Perdita was along on the sleeper, the next minute she had disappeared in a whirling mass of grey and white bodies and thrashing wings. To say I was alarmed was putting it mildly. I'd seen birds mobbed before but I'd never known so many gulls set upon another bird with such fury.

I had a friend with me and we both waded in to get her. We went deeper and deeper until we were standing in about four feet of water, flailing our arms about to scare away the gulls. Pecked, clawed, thrashed by dozens of wings and unable to defend herself, Perdita had been beaten down on the sleeper. I grabbed her, fighting off the screaming gulls that turned their attack on me, and carried her away. It wasn't until we were on firm ground again that I realised how lucky it was that Perdita had been in comparatively shallow water; in some of the lakes the ground disappeared suddenly in great holes twenty or thirty feet deep.

Perdita was wet, muddy and frightened. I wanted to get her straight home and decided to go the short way, tackling a steep slope that was far from easy going in decent weather. The weather *hadn't* been decent, there'd been a great deal of rain and my pal and I were soaked, anyway, squelching and dripping, struggling upwards on ground that had the consistency of porridge. All the time I was trying to keep my balance with a large, dejected bird a dead weight on my fist.

When we were halfway up the sheer idiocy of our situation occured to us. I laugh easily, anyway, at my own and everyone else's; we were almost at the top when I let out a shout of laughter, lost my footing and skidded back down the slope, face first in the mud, my left arm stuck rigidly out at an angle. Perdita, squawking furiously, was still clinging to me when I landed at the bottom in three feet of muddy water.

Some little time later Pat, opening the front door, murmured something about 'the elegant and romantic tradition of hawking' as two mud-plastered men carrying a wrecked-looking bird tramped past her into the kitchen.

Once Perdita was flying free Kit often went along for company – and possibly light relief. Pegged down by the end of his leash he would interestedly watch Perdita doing her stint until it was his turn, then Pat flew him while I carried Perdita. That was the routine, and it worked very well. Until Kit sabotaged it.

After she had flown, Perdita perched on my fist, savouring her reward – on this occasion a large chicken head. Pat cast Kit off and we watched him soar up, Perdita meanwhile ignoring everything and brooding to herself over the tasty morsel she was about to enjoy.

She never did. Kit had seen the chicken head, too, and he loved them. With his incredible swiftness he switched from a hover to a full-speed stoop and – before my utterly disbelieving eyes – shot behind Perdita, underneath her, zipped up between her legs and grabbed the chicken head.

Perdita grabbed, too, and she got him. But only just. The tactic had startled her as much as it had amazed me. Kit's wings were free. Weighed down as he was with his prize – which he refused to relinquish – he made a convulsive wrench for his freedom, and his life, spurting out of Perdita's claw like toothpaste squeezed from a tube. He left his tail behind – or, rather, the pigeon feathers that served as his tail. Not that that mattered, I could always provide him with more.

I knew Kit. I knew that having once got away with such an audacious theft he would try it again, he wouldn't be able to resist it, and a second time he couldn't possibly be so lucky. So I always flew him first after that, taking no chances; I didn't want to lose my beloved kestrel to an outraged Perdita.

Five

The owl with no name

Thing. He deliberately didn't have a name. He was a magnificent barn owl and his history, as far as I could trace it, was that he had been taken – very young and illegally – from his nest and reared as a pet. Now, he was to be returned to the wild and with this intention the less notice anyone took of him the better.

Whoever had kept him had found the trouble of looking after him too much. By rather devious means he had passed from them to someone else and then on to the RSPCA, who had kept him for a short while until, optimistically imagining him to be ready to go free, they took him along to some woods and turned him loose. They watched him flutter up into a tree and perch there. Satisfied, they returned to their van and started the engine. Just as they were about to drive off a mighty clunking noise made them leap out.

Thing was sitting on top of the van. He belonged with human beings, he knew that, even if they didn't.

Two or three times they put him up in a tree, each time the performance was repeated. When they tried to leave Thing clung to them, he wasn't going anywhere on his own. Eventually, acknowledging defeat, they brought him to me, knowing from past experience that I had the patience and the determination, and the time, to rehabilitate the owl.

Thing didn't go in the outside aviary. For such a thoroughly humanised owl there was far too much going on there – we were regularly cleaning up and feeding the birds, visitors were always in and out of the yard, the window of the house – and whoever happened to be inside it – was always in sight. The

51

house itself, of course, was out of the question. But the house next door, I decided, would serve the purpose well enough. Pat's father lived alone there. He was able to get about a little during the day but the owl wouldn't trouble him then. The spare bedroom was unoccupied and he had no objection to our making use of it.

The owl was diurnal, but he had to learn to adapt himself to nocturnal habits, as nature intended. During the day he lived in the bedroom. At night, Pat went in and saw her father settled, then she shut his bedroom door, opened all the other doors, left food for Thing, switched off all the lights and went away.

Stealthy as a ghost, the barn owl prowled away the nights in the silent house. I got up very early in the mornings and it was my routine to make tea and nip next door with a cup for Pat's father. He was usually awake and, more often than not, inclined to be querulous. One morning when I went in he began a rambling, incoherent complaint.

At least, it was incoherent to me. I said, 'What? What?' without getting anywhere. I was always in a hurry, there was a lot to do and half past five wasn't the ideal time to make sense of an old man's preoccupations. 'I haven't *time* – tell Pat –' I said, putting down the cup and saucer and rushing out.

When I got back into our house I took Pat up her cup of tea. 'Your father's complaining about something.'

'Is he all right?' she asked.

'Oh, he's all *right*. He's just complaining.' We were both accustomed to her father's irascibility.

'Never mind,' Pat said soothingly. 'I'll go in and see directly I get up.'

When she did, the old man came straight to the point. 'That thing's kept me awake all night,' he quavered. 'You left my door open.'

Thing, intrigued to come upon human company – even if it was prone and uncommunicative – had whiled away the night fluttering across the old man's room, walking about on his bed, or simply sitting on the bed-head staring down at him.

In the early hours of the morning I seldom had time to bother with Thing. I went in and out so fast he could hardly take in that I was there at all. It was Pat, going in later, who steadfastly ignored any friendly overtures and shoo'd Thing upstairs to his own room and shut the door on him. After a while Thing understood that upstairs was his barn and he must return there as soon as it grew light. Going in and looking around carefully, not daring to call him or make any sound that would encourage him to fly to her, Pat would eventually go upstairs and find him perched somewhere in the room, looking at her with his enormous, sad eyes. She could shut him in and get on with cleaning up any mess he might have made before she began to attend to her father.

This routine established, she grew to rely on it. One morning something happened to distract her, she had to go out straightaway to the yard and, knowing that the owl would already be upstairs, she unthinkingly left the door open. After a while she turned from what she was doing and looked towards the kitchen. The owl was perched on top of the open door.

Brief as her morning visit was he'd grown accustomed to it; because she had neglected to go in, glance at him and shut the door, he'd flown downstairs to look for her. Having found her, he sat patiently waiting for her.

In the evening, when I came home from work, she told me what had happened. 'He made no attempt to fly away. He should have done, but he didn't. Our programme isn't working, is it?'

I agreed that it wasn't, that something else must be done 'We'll keep him in the bedroom all the time, with the minimum of human contact. And we'll even feed him in the dark.'

It was a good idea. After a couple of trial runs Pat grew so adept at finding her way round in the dark she sometimes wondered if she might not be turning into a nocturnal creature herself. Some sort of hybrid . . . *The Owl-feeding Batwoman, a rare mammal of quiet but curious habits. Occasionally sighted in Levenshulme. Knits a lot . . .*

But one night some movement she made startled Thing. He flew swiftly across the room, too low, and collided with her, snatching at her hair for an instant before launching himself to fly on. She felt the rake of his claws on her scalp and forehead and by the time she got downstairs the blood was pouring down her face.

. . . for reasons not understood by naturalists, the Batwoman exposes herself to attack by owls and is in danger of extinction.

That was an accident, but it was true that as time went by Thing began increasingly to resent any chance disturbance during the day. Pat had to go in sometimes to clean up the room, causing him a displeasure he expressed by making a muttering noise. If she stayed too long he sidled into the curtain until it was draped around him, and from this hiding place he grumbled at her until she went away.

At last I was convinced that the owl was ready to go. There was nothing to be gained by keeping him any longer in isolation. He was a splendid, strong young bird with many years to live out his life as it should be lived. One evening, while it was still light, I went next door with a cardboard box and after a slight tussle succeeded in getting the owl into it. Then we drove out to some property that belonged to a farmer friend.

The farmer's children were there, waiting for us, slightly apprehensive but thoroughly excited to get a glimpse of this fierce creature before it sped away forever. Remembering the damage Thing had done to Pat, and afraid that it might fly at the children and frighten them, I warned them to keep well away. I herded them together at a little distance, telling them to stand still. 'We must be very quiet. He's a wild bird and we don't want to startle him, do we?'

Pat, meanwhile, opened the lid of the box and put her hand inside to shoo Thing out. A moment later, her face a picture of comic resignation, she was standing with the owl perched on her wrist – an owl whose manner was so unmistakably docile he might have been waiting for weeks just for this chance of making friends with her.

'Bob . . .' she wailed. 'He's at it again . . .'

The children clutched their sides with glee. A tiny one, delighted by the sight of the beautiful, gentle toy on Pat's wrist, crooned softly, 'Oooh . . . Thing . . . Thing.'

54

I swore under my breath.

'Well, I *refuse* to take him back. Not again. He'll think it's some kind of game.'

'Maybe it is,' Pat said, with some sarcasm, as Thing sidled amiably up her arm and sat on her shoulder.

Determined to deal with the owl once and for all, we continued with our original intention – to set him at liberty in the barn. He was used to being indoors, he was used to being fed, too, but hunger would drive him to catch the mice and rats in which the place abounded. He could sleep by day and hunt by night, and when he chose to go free all he had to do was fly into the dense woods bordering the farm.

In procession, we trooped to the barn, adults, owl, children. Inside, Pat took Thing on her hand and deliberately cast him off. He swooped and glided, alighting at last, quite close to us, on a bale of hay. The bale at once took his attention, he found there were more and he hopped and fluttered about, rooting amongst them, emerging every so often to have a look at us.

We began a gradual retreat while he was busy examining his new territory. He was so busy, in fact, that quite suddenly he didn't notice, or didn't care, that we were abandoning him. Pat had a last glimpse of him, the gliding creamy-white of his body as he soared high up into the roof, wheeling, alighting on a beam, settling into the stillness of his ancient calm, merging into the shadows, waiting for the night.

For some time afterwards we called or phoned regularly to see how he was taking to his new freedom. He lived for a while in the barn and the children went regularly to visit him, very early in the morning, before he took himself off somewhere to sleep. Gradually he grew more and more aloof as the distance between his life and the life of human beings lengthened; then one day they could not find him at all, he had flown away.

Thing had at last understood he was owl.

The telephone rings constantly, sometimes with the curtest requests from strangers who obviously have no manners and consider people who deal with birds haven't either. 'I've got an injured bird here. Come and collect it . . .' 'I've been told you take in birds. You'd better come for this one . . .' And once, astoundingly, a voice that said, 'You're the bird man, aren't you? I'm having a party, will you bring an owl along.'

'Will I what?' I asked, bewildered.

'Bring an owl. As a gimmick.'

No longer bewildered, I told him, comprehensively, how he could conduct his parties. The man rang off before I'd finished.

I have a definite aversion to animals and birds being used in any way for the entertainment of human beings. If birds have their own idiosyncrasies and wish to adopt engaging habits – that's up to them, I would neither encourage nor coerce them in any way; I believe in training but I don't believe in tricks, there's a world of difference between the two. Animals have a natural dignity, they retain it when they're trained to do work in harmony with their temperaments and capabilities and, as we take dogs and cats to live in our houses, it is entirely reasonable to encourage them to be clean; but to teach them tricks, to use them as clowns, is a distortion of their dignity.

It's because I have this attitude that I was very unwilling once to agree to a suggestion from an animal aid society that we take a bird along to help raise funds at a charity fair that was being held locally. In fact, I said no straightaway. Pat took the opposite view. 'Oh, come on, it's all in a good cause, and no one's asking it to *perform*. Forget your principles just this once.'

She had her way, and Barney went to the fair. He sat on a log with devastating solemnity and did absolutely nothing at all. Simply by being there he was a focus of attention. Pat stayed beside him and whenever people gathered round to look at him and say, 'Aaah, an owl, isn't it lovely?' she picked up the collecting box and rattled it at them. Very occasionally, Barney assisted by putting one claw carefully on the box, if only, Pat was convinced, to stop her making such a damned row. Nevertheless, she smiled her winning smile and said, 'That's right, shake your box at all these nice people, Barney.'

The combination of her absolute cheek and her charm – plus Barney's – paid off. They collected twenty pounds.

One evening we had a phone call from a man who explained

that three weeks previously his wife had found a rare bird lying in the garden. She'd picked it up, thinking it was dead, and taken it in the house to have a closer look at it; when she did, she found that it was still alive.

'A rare bird,' I said, my eyes lighting up. 'Do you know what it is?'

'Well, no. Something tropical, I think. It's been hurt, its head, mainly – but it seems not to be bothered –'

The difficulty, however, was that the man's wife, wishing to keep the bird, had converted the garage to its exclusive use, which meant that the car had to stand outside all the time. And not only that, the bird ate a lot, they couldn't afford to go on keeping it. Would I take it off their hands?

Of course I would. The man gave me his address and it was a fair way to travel but I was excited at the prospect of having a rare bird to look after and didn't mind the distance. Unusual birds do turn up, without rhyme or reason, in the most unlikely places. It's something that up till then I'd heard of but never had the luck to experience myself except on two occasions when, unluckily, the birds had already died and were brought to my notice as a matter of interest. Both were found in Manchester, in the centre of the city. One was a Firecrest, a tiny, pretty bird that has been known to breed in very small numbers in the southern half of England but, as far as I know, never ventures north. The other was a Little Auk, a sea bird that is seen in the extreme north, round the Shetland Isles, but is habitually very remote, living out in ice-bound seas.

In this instance, however, when I did arrive it was to be met with something of a let-down: the bird was a jay. Certainly, it was handsome, and with its vivid colouring likely to mislead anyone who didn't know into thinking it was a rarity. It had obviously been in an accident, its head was out of shape, as if it had been crushed.

The man, objecting initially to being deprived of the use of his garage, grew to object even more to the jay's appetite. His wife, not knowing what type of bird it was, had tried feeding it on the most likely and unlikely things. Eventually, as much by chance as anything else, she discovered it had a taste for best steak, raw; the cost of providing this was exorbitant, adding up – per week – to more than the amount the two spent on themselves for meat. Basil, the jay, had to go.

And as it had nowhere else to go, it went with me. I intended to keep it for a while to see if it made a complete recovery, then release it. When I got it home I put it in the cage under the stairs to live with the mynah birds. But Basil did not live very long, for he developed (or had possibly arrived with) a skin infection. With alarming rapidity his feathers began to fall out and his skin blistered and peeled. I treated him with antibiotic powder as a temporary measure until I could get to the source of the trouble, but before I could discover what might account for Basil's condition, the jay died. The mynahs, sharing the same cage, weren't affected at all and I never did find out what the infection was.

It was one mouth less to feed amongst the many, and when it came to the cost of it all I knew how the woman's husband had felt. Out of my own pocket I meet every single expense: medical care, equipment, transportation and food. If I had to pay for all the food consumed the cost would be beyond me and many birds would be turned away; but I have friends – and they, fortunately, have friends – ready to contribute a share of their hunting parties – hares, pigeons, rabbits.

I couldn't, however, rely on getting food day by day or week by week – I have to stock up, and in those days that meant cramming every inch of space in the fridge. Many a time Pat went to the fridge and searched unavailingly amongst the carcases for something for us to eat, emerging defeated. 'Bob, there's nothing for dinner. I'll have to go to the shops. Again.'

Thinking it over one day, she decided she might as well make use of her father's fridge next door, as his food took up very little room and, in fact, he seldom attended to his own domestic arrangements, she saw to everything for him. Once she started using his fridge I did, too, but unfortunately, I forgot to tell anyone . . . then the old man opened the door one day and a fox fell out on him.

He had grumbled for days about the owl in his bedroom; it took him weeks to get over the fox.

'I don't know why he keeps complaining,' I said to Pat. 'After all, it was dead.'

The fox had been killed by a car, someone had brought it to me late at night, asking if it was any use. 'Certainly,' I said, but our fridge was full. Then I thought of the one next door; the old man was in bed and need not be disturbed, and in the morning, as usual, I was in a tearing hurry and forgot . . .

'What was he doing at the fridge, anyway?' I asked.

'Well, it is *his*,' Pat pointed out. She was getting tired of being the Aunt Sally for her menfolks' grievances. 'We'll have to buy a freezer, that's the only answer. I know they're expensive, but we'll just have to afford it.'

'Yes,' I agreed. 'A big one.'

'Yes. Er . . . Where will we keep it?' – the scullery was tiny.

'In the front room, of course,' I said. 'When you're not working in it it never gets used.'

The next day we went out and bought the biggest freezer we could find. The salesman went on at great length about the many and varied uses of a freezer; this one was so versatile I began to wonder if it played tunes. 'There's no end,' he said, 'to the things you can keep in it.'

'We want it for food for our birds,' Pat said sweetly. The salesman, open-mouthed, and no doubt imagining we intended to fill it with seed, looked at her as if she was mad. Pat didn't care, she'd got a freezer for the birds, and her own fridge back again.

Pat always wanted a garden, too, but her efforts in that direction were continually frustrated. A plot of ground was out of the question, there simply wasn't room; but she thought of a compromise – a short, low wall with a cavity that could be filled with earth, she could grow things in that.

I built the wall. But it was a pity I built it along the side of the aviary. Pat had a modest dream of being able to look out of the window into the yard and see flowers blooming along the top of the wall. Instead, what she could see was the birds sticking their beaks through the netting and pulling up anything that was growing. Anything.

She went on trying for a long time but eventually she had to give up. As always with her, defeat is tempered by good humour: she bought a bunch of plastic flowers and stuck them in the earth along the wall. 'Go on,' she said to the birds, 'just try and swallow those.'

Then a neighbour offered to give her some rooted cuttings of a climbing plant, one that was guaranteed to be tough enough to grow anywhere and take the roughest treatment; in fact, once it got going, it could be a *nuisance* . . .

Delighted with the idea of a plant actually being hardy enough to be a nuisance, Pat accepted eagerly. She chose the tiniest area just outside the aviary, broke up the ground, carefully prepared it and put in the cuttings. It was a place difficult for the birds to get at and by the time the plant had taken hold and was climbing up the netting it would be vigorous enough to withstand a little pecking. Feeling she was winning at last, she watered and tended the cuttings as they struggled to establish themselves.

Every so often the buzzards have a 'day out' in the aviary. One morning I took them down before I went to work. For some reason Pat was particularly busy that day and didn't go into the yard until the evening, then we both went out to bring the buzzards in. As soon as we stepped into the yard Pat said, 'Oh, no . . . Look –'

Where the other birds had ignored the cuttings, Perdita and Horus had done their worst. They'd managed to reach them, dragged out every one and scattered them about the aviary to lie all day, exposed and unsustained. Pat picked up one shrivelled specimen, dangling it by its torn, flaccid leaf, remembering how the neighbour had said, '*Nothing* can kill these.'

' – except buzzards,' Pat murmured, resigned.

She had some early success with a rose tree in a tub, the tub on which Hootie the owl had waited for us to nod at him from the window. That was before there were so many birds, and by the time Hootie chose it as his perch the rose tree was in its death throes. After the wall and the buzzards, Pat rescued the tub from the aviary, put it in the yard and planted a new tree. Then we had an unexpected arrival, as much as anything in the house can be called unexpected – or, as Pat said gravely to a visitor one night, 'We've just acquired a new bird. A *gallus domesticus . . .*'

In other words, a hen. Clara Cluck, a great cushion of a bird, absorbed in her own impenetrable, amiable stupidity, was the victim of a road accident, although what she'd been doing in the road at all no one could fathom. It seemed she'd just been wandering about when she'd been hit by a bus.

Now, many a bird couldn't survive an encounter with a bicycle, but Clara had one of those charmed lives, its predominant characteristic being a blundering preoccupation with pecking and scratching and *positively nothing else*. She went under the bus and came out the other end of it, a bit plucked-looking, a few scratches here and there and presumably concussed beyond the point where she could actively scratch, although her claws were making feeble movements indicative of the intention.

She came to us through an animal charity with whom the police had been in touch. The story of her 'apprehension' was not at all clear, there were conflicting accounts of her being picked up . . . approaching a policeman . . . or was it a police station? I wouldn't be surprised. I think she gave herself up, and certainly no one ever went looking for her and reported her missing.

By the time we got her she'd completely recovered from her concussion and when we looked at her we could find nothing wrong with her apart from one or two small scars and a rather bald bottom. However, we decided she'd better stay indoors for a day or two so we could keep an eye on her, during which time she wreaked havoc with her incessant pecking and scratching. Pat was in despair about the carpet – not that Clara confined her attentions to that, she raked over the cushions on the armchairs and settee and was all set to have the linoleum up, given time. Which she wasn't, out into the yard went Clara.

'Thank God,' Pat breathed. But she'd forgotten her rose tree.

Obligingly, Clara paid for her keep by regularly laying eggs for us in the little straw-filled hutch we'd made for her, where she could wander in and out as she pleased. One day, when Pat looked out of the window, she was in the tub, flinging the earth up in showers, destroying the rose tree with single-minded enthusiasm.

Regularly, Pat walks down the road to the shops and back again. Sometimes, when she gets to the house, she meets a neighbour and they stand on the pavement for a few moments, talking. Then, whether she wants to or not, something forces her to turn her head and look at the windows. And there they are, upstairs and down, the bright reproachful eyes, staring fixedly at her. The birds, hearing her voice, wait anxiously for her, not daring – it seems – to release her from their gaze, in case she goes away again. And forgets to come back.

Six

Jeannie

We had another kestrel. It had been with us some time; we didn't take it out flying with Kit and Perdita, though, because it couldn't fly. Much later, when it was well and happy and bossing all the birds in the house, I would look at it in a faintly wondering way, amazed that it was alive at all.

The RSPCA had called me one evening to say that some people had found a bird in their garden and didn't know what to do with it. Would I go along and have a look?

I went, and despairingly brought the kestrel away. I've learnt, slowly and sometimes very bitterly, not to ask questions. If people wanted to explain the circumstances under which they had come by a bird, they would. If they wanted to tell a pack of lies they would do that, too, and I had no way of sorting out truth from fiction. Whenever possible I tried to pass on some of my knowledge of caring for birds, and sometimes this advice was accepted, sometimes it was turned aside. As a plain man who speaks plainly I came to understand the necessity of hanging on to my temper and saving my energies for doing something practical.

On this occasion I could get nowhere in discovering what could possibly account for the condition of the kestrel. The only sensible course was to pick it up and bring it away.

I don't think I've ever seen anything in such a state. Its wings appeared to have been broken and set again in a strangely distorted way. Its back was twisted; one leg was withered, the other broken, and someone had set it in a splint and plaster but clumsily, with the result that the claw stuck out sideways. All these injuries rendered it completely helpless; it had been lying

63

on the ground so long its chest had split and the bone was protruding.

When I got home with it I said, 'It's no good, Trish, look at the state it's in, God knows how it got like this. I'll have to kill it, I don't know why it hasn't died already, it probably will soon, anyway.'

But Pat fed it. She fed everything. It was almost a conditioned reflex with her – see a beak, push food in it. The poor damaged creature ate and looked for more. To Pat the proposition was simple: if it wanted to eat it wanted to live, and we would try to help it if we could.

We removed the splint from the broken leg – it was doing no good anyway as the leg had already set. About the strange, crooked shape in which it had set we could do nothing (I could possibly have broken the leg and re-set it but I wouldn't consider doing anything to put the bird to further distress). The odd little claws, sticking out at an angle, appeared to be capable of some movement but had no power in them at all. There was no question of putting the bird out into the aviary, it was unable to do anything at all for itself so it had to stay in the house.

It was in the house that Pat carried him about with her, talking to him as she did her housework. If she had slides to prepare she would take him in the front room, where she did her lab work, and put him on top of the heater. Warm and contented, the invalid kept her company, watching her with his bright, inquisitive eyes. Occasionally, if she had to leave him for some reason, she put him in a large cage. The two cats were completely friendly but as he was so small, and quite immobile, there was the danger he might be intimidated by their presence if Pat was not there to push their exploring noses out of the way.

Right from the beginning he had a tremendous appetite. When she left him he would set up a plaintive squeaking noise, demanding her attention until she went to him, fed him, and then returned to whatever she was doing. Whenever she had any spare time she would sit with him on her lap, massaging his legs. She spent hours doing this; his twisted beak seemed to make his entire head look awry and as he lay staring up at her, his eyes bright in his dishevelled little face, she'd murmur to him, 'You are a funny boo-bird, aren't you?' The description suited his eager, droll expression; shortened, it attached itself to him as his name: Boo.

At night he slept in a cage in the back bedroom. Sometimes we had to be out for quite long periods of time and Pat wouldn't leave him on his own. She had a feeling – difficult to put into words – that if he was deprived of the comfort and encouragement of her presence, he would suffer. So wherever we went he went with us, travelling in his cage.

After a time we noticed that the use was returning to his legs. At first he could only lurch about at ground level, his wings still being of no use to him at all. Then he began to hop. Once he found he could do that he seemed continually to be looking for places to hop to, so to encourage him we put obstacles for him to tackle, building up small boxes in a series of steps until he could climb up on to a chair.

With all this exercise his wings grew stronger as he brought them into use to propel and balance himself, although they'd set hopelessly out of shape and nothing could be done about that. His back, too, always remained twisted, throwing his tail out at a curious angle. But in spite of these drawbacks, Boo was not beaten. He progressed from hopping to fluttering, to launching himself off from the boxes, then from the chair. Then he was flying again, really flying: swooping with great gusto from the curtain pelmet to the rail above the kitchen door, into the front room and the scullery, finding his way upstairs to the bedroom.

He was all the wrong shape and he should have been dead; but he lived for years, an affectionate little tyrant. Possibly because of all the attention he had received when he had been so injured, he considered he had exclusive rights on us and was always furiously jealous of other birds. For a while there were times when it was necessary to put him in the outdoor aviary. He resented this wildly, refusing to reconcile himself to being banished and sulking and squabbling all the time. When Pat had to go into the yard he flung himself at the wire, clinging to it, threshing his wings and making a terrible clamour.

She would look at him, half laughing at the way he appeared

to be trying to convince her that something absolutely terrible was happening to him in the aviary and if she didn't rescue him it would soon be Too Late. 'I know you . . . you're having me on,' she'd say to him. But, all the same, he'd grown so accustomed to being with her, and grown to accept the house – not the aviary – as his rightful place . . .

So eventually we took him back into the house and he stayed there, ordering the other birds about with his irate *tchk-tchk-tchk*; scrutinising visitors with enormous self-possession; establishing who was boss by making a point of always being the first to steal the food from unwary newcomers. Alert, inquisitive, ready to defend his territory, he glared down from his favourite perch over the kitchen door on that autumn evening when our next weird, dirty, half-plucked creature emerged from the tea-chest to begin its life all over again.

Of course, she wasn't called Jeannie at first, and she was scarcely recognisable as anything very much – just a collapsed sort of creature in a tea-chest carried by two rather puzzled policemen.

We were pretty crowded in the kitchen, what with us, the policemen, the tea-chest, and the Siamese cats. And there were some owls and several other kestrels about, being aloof or inquisitive, depending on their temperaments; as it was evening and close to supper time they were mostly just hungry, anyway. With the anxiety of creatures whose routine is in danger of disruption, their imperious, wild little faces looked down from perches, bookcases, the backs of chairs – at us, and we were giving all our attention to the thing in the tea-chest.

It looked like a roughly plucked chicken, but very much larger: skin and prickles and a splodgy shape, dirty and cowed, squatting at the bottom of the chest. 'What is it?' the policemen wanted to know. Pat looked at me, echoing the question, 'What is it?'

'I'm not sure . . .' I said.

How could anyone tell what the peculiar, half bald thing was? The policemen were merely transporting her from the airport, all they knew of her was the manner in which she had been transported, they could not help in the matter of where she had come from in the first place. They had to leave then, their curiosity unsatisfied, and when they had gone I sat and considered and realised that as I had no idea where the bird had come from . . . I had virtually the whole world to guess at.

Carefully, I took her from the chest and looked at her. She was big, certainly one of the biggest birds I'd ever had, but extremely thin. This could have been accounted for by her build as well as starvation – certainly the latter contributed to her evident exhaustion.

In her bristly state she would have been comical if she hadn't been so pathetic. Here and there a few feathers had escaped shearing and stuck out in brave little blurs of colour. Her face was obviously much paler than her body, her beak enormous and hooked; her legs and feet, too, were massive, seeming out of proportion with the rest of her. On the undersides of her claws were a series of hooks, or spikes, and these I knew were characteristic of all fish-eating birds of prey. Gently, I spread her wings out. All the primary and secondary feathers had been hacked off but the wing itself had the odd cranked shape typical of fishing birds such as the osprey. But I would have recognised an osprey, even in that state, so she wasn't one of those.

Pat ventured an opinion that she might be a kite. The colour of the stubby bits of feathers the bird had retained, her general shape and the obvious fact that she was a hawk of some kind suggested this. The kite, an uncommon bird, has a most distinctive tail – but as this bird's tail feathers had been removed entirely that aid to identification had gone, too.

'We won't know anything until she gets some plumage,' I said. 'Anyway, whatever she is, she's here, we'd better see what we can do for her . . .'

She was too weak to eat, we had to open her beak and push the food in. It was a beak designed by nature as a ferocious weapon; the huge claws, too, were obviously meant to squeeze and kill and rip. But the bird was not inclined to aggression, she was simply not interested in anything.

I put jesses on her straight away. This was merely a pre-caution and would assist me in handling her in the future; as she was, she let me do anything. Her stunned state was natur-ally accounted for by the conditions under which she had lived for probably several days. She had no detectable injuries, if there was anything more wrong with her – and, as it turned out, there was – nothing was immediately apparent.

She spent the night in the spare bedroom, perched on a log, fastened by a leash to her jesses. In the morning she was still un-able, or disinclined, to eat; we force-fed her again and put her in the aviary. By then the aviary was pretty crowded, she was an unknown quantity and we couldn't be sure how she would react to the other birds. To be on the safe side we kept the leash at-tached to her jesses – which was what we did with the buzzards, who attacked the other birds, given half a chance.

As I've said before, we're early risers, we have to be. As well as the normal domestic tasks of every day, there were the birds and cats to feed and clean up after, I had to get off to work and Pat had to busy herself looking after two houses and her invalid father.

If anything goes wrong, fate generally arranges that it goes wrong *after* I've left for work. That morning, when Pat went out to the yard, she saw that in the aviary the strange bird was lying on its side. Its eyes were open and it was obviously alive but it was absolutely quiet and strangely stiff.

Puzzled, Pat picked it up, handled it a little and set it on its feet. As it appeared to be all right, she fed it again and left it. Occasionally, in the past she had known birds react against being jessed and she thought that possibly this might have something to do with the odd incident.

Later in the day she went out again, and again the bird was lying on the ground. She couldn't tell how long it had been there, she could only go through the same procedure as before, picking up and setting it right.

When I came home from work the bird appeared to be quite normal but, of course, Pat told me what had happened. For years the life we'd led inured us to the unexpected, we talked over this strange behaviour and tried to make some sense of it.

It sounded to me as if the bird suffered from fits of some kind; I knew from my reading that this did happen although it wasn't within my personal experience. I suggested we watch her carefully and take note of her behaviour – 'But just to be going on with, we know what her symptoms are so far, we'll get out the books and do some research.'

A little later, uneasy, I went out and brought the bird into the kitchen. I knew she was a juvenile, as much by instinct as the evidence of her few scraps of feathers – apart from that I knew very little about her. What worried me principally was that I still hadn't been able to pinpoint what was wrong – the books had been of no help there – and could do nothing for her. Apathetically, she perched on the back of the settee, ignoring the inquisitive advances of the cats and Boo's noisy demands for her attention. We left her and busied ourselves with things we had to do.

Suddenly, without any warning, the bird let out the most frightful, piercing scream and collapsed.

She dropped as if she had been felled by a powerful blow. By the time I reached her she was lying on her side on the floor behind the sofa, absolutely rigid, her muscles as solid as bars of iron, her wings outflung, her legs and feet locked.

Birds have a transparent 'third eyelid' called a nictating membrane that draws across the eye when the bird blinks or sleeps; I saw that this membrane had closed over her eyes. Pat, bending forward to look, saw this too, and said, 'I don't think it was like that before. I think it was open.'

'That's it, then, she's dead . . .' I said. But as I touched the bird I felt the beat of her heart, the membrane began to open again and she made the slightest movement, more a vibration of her body. Gently, as I picked her up, I tried to close her stiffly outflung wings. She gave a weird, high scream and I stopped. When I tried to move her legs the same thing happened.

The cats, disturbed, prowled uneasily about. Boo complained vociferously; the mynahs whistled. It was not exactly a restful atmosphere for a bird emerging from a seizure. 'Give her to me,' Pat said. 'I'll take her in the hall.'

There were no distractions there and Pat – knowing that

69

birds grow quiet in the dark, being comforted by it – did not switch on the light. There wasn't much room, either, just enough for her, the coat-stand and the chair I took out for her. Fortunately, no one came to the door during the time she was there and she stayed a long while, sitting in the dark, massaging the bird's legs, its clenched claws, its tense wings, until they relaxed and movement returned to them.

That fit had lasted fifteen minutes, not that we timed it then, being too concerned about caring for the bird. But we had adequate opportunity as the days and weeks went by to measure the duration and regularity of each fit. After that first evening, every hour – on the hour, day and night – Jeannie took a screaming plunge into oblivion.

Her limbs, massaged back to use again, would sometimes jerk involuntarily as the life returned, the talons raking deep gashes across our hands. When she was sensible again she was fed or given medicine, or both, then she would lie or perch quietly somewhere while the clock crept round to another hour.

Pat's painstaking research, plus the chance advice of a medical friend who happened to call, uncovered one source of Jeannie's illness – a severe deficiency of Vitamin B. That meant that at least we could treat her with medicine and tablets and she was also on a very high protein diet; for the rest, it was simply care, patience and determination.

But it was a nerve-wracking period. Looking back on it later we sometimes wondered how, with the sleeplessness and the strain, we remained on speaking terms. However, imperceptibly, the time between the seizures was lengthening. One hour became two, two hours became three . . . In the intervals, Jeannie's apathy turned to an agreeable docility, then to interest.

Her feet were massive, her legs ridiculously long; her thin body, on top of them, sprouted its bristly feathers. Looking like a badly designed hedgehog on stilts she took walks along chairs or pottered about the floor with the cats. She found she could squeak, an absurd sound, faint at first, with echoes of untraceable alarm, then growing stronger as she discovered the response was invariably Pat's attention.

'You look like nothing on earth,' Pat said to her. 'And I'm busy, I've got things to do.'

But Jeannie went on squeaking, she knew by then that Pat couldn't ignore her for long.

Someone, hearing of Jeannie's terrible condition and the effort it had taken to bring her back to health, once asked, 'Why didn't you just kill it?'

The answer – if there is an answer at all – can only be: why not kill everything that's sick?

Seven

A Victorian maiden on a chaise-longue

Early one summer a group of young people holidaying on a barge on the canal near Preston saw a large bird floundering on marshland. They went to investigate and found a heron, in great distress, flopping and falling about. They managed to pick her up, handling the frightened bird as gently as they could, and with the thought of getting help for her they contacted a vet, who declined to treat her. Not prepared to give up so easily they phoned a friend who lived in a town in Cheshire, some nine or ten miles from us. The friend, who had some contact with animal welfare, thought he might be able to help and suggested they sail their barge down the canal to meet him the next day.

From that point ensued a complicated series of phone calls, messages, suggestions, attempts to help, offers of assistance – the heron meanwhile passing from hand to hand – until somebody said they knew somebody who had heard of 'a bird man'. That was my cue. I didn't concern myself with the ramifications of who had done what, where or when. I know that when an injured bird needs help it needs it *at once*; so I was there, with Pat, wrapping up in a towel a creature that looked like a broken-stringed marionette and taking it home.

We laid her out on the settee. There was so little sign of life in her it seemed our effort and journey had been just wasted time, but once again Pat's instinct took over. There were occasions when she had to admit there was no hope, and she would be the first to see that a creature went gently from life when life was insupportable to it; but this time, from a conviction she could never rationalise, she said to me, 'We've got to try.' And that was what we did.

We arranged the heron as comfortably as possible, placing a cushion beneath her head to keep it slightly raised to permit the flow of saliva down her throat. Having no fish in the house I settled for the next best thing – strips of meat soaked in water – and fed them into her beak. Afterwards, we had a look at her.

She was a very young bird, in fact she still had her downy juvenile plumage. It was obvious that starvation was her trouble, and there was a specific cause.

At some time one of her legs had been broken. It had healed, but imperfectly – we could see where it had reset and in doing so had overlapped. This meant that the leg was about an inch and a half shorter than the other and the foot was twisted outwards. The break had very probably happened in the nest, herons can be quite clumsy creatures; it would have set while she was still there and, of course, her parents would have been feeding her all that time.

But once she left the nest it was a different matter. She could not stalk anything in the water. When she put down her shortened leg its splayed foot did not glide – as nature had designed – instead it splashed, giving warning of her approach and startling away the fish that were her prey. For too long she had caught barely enough to keep herself alive. Probably she had fed off worms and beetles until eventually her weakened condition had rendered her completely helpless and she had collapsed into the state in which she was found.

At home with us she lay for three weeks on the settee, unable to move of her own accord, languid as a Victorian maiden on a chaise-longue. She ate readily enough, though, and we wanted to make sure she was getting the correct amount, not too little or – equally important – not too much. As I was not sure of the quantity she required I contacted Peter Grayson, the manager of Belle Vue Zoo, who later became a good friend and source of help. Peter advised us and also managed to procure some food for the heron, whom we'd christened Henrietta.

Although she was not able to move or feed herself for such a long time Henrietta was not completely immobile or unresponsive. Pat picked her up regularly during the course of the day, holding her over newspapers half an hour after each feed to enable her to clear her bowels. Every time she stood her up she encouraged the heron to take a few steps, holding her round her body and persuading her to walk a little way. At first this was beyond the bird but gradually, as Pat patiently stuck to this routine, she began to take a few steps. When she grew tired she would lift both her feet from the ground and Pat suddenly found herself supporting a great deal of heron – with the job of carting it back to the settee.

For a wild creature all this handling could have caused a distress sufficient to fret the bird until the object of the care itself was defeated, and at first Henrietta had been too near death to care what happened to her, but as she began to revive it was plain she had developed complete trust in Pat. A heron's nine inch long stiletto of a beak is a fearsome weapon; putting it close to Pat's face, Henrietta took to making a curious croaking noise in her throat that sounded to the uninitiated as if she was clacking her beak.

Pat sensed there was no hostility in the bird, that she was, in fact, just 'talking'. But a friend who called one day was alarmed at this procedure, warning Pat of the danger of being within range of the long, ferocious beak. 'I'm all right,' Pat said mildly, above the sound of staccato clacking. 'She's not threatening me. She's making conversation.'

Henrietta's recovery was slow. It was eight weeks before she could stand and walk by herself. Once she was strong enough she left the settee and pottered about on the floor, making no attempt to fly because her wings were useless. Initially, there were two reasons for this; one was that she was far too weak, the other was her juvenile feathers. She was very late in getting her adult plumage, probably the set-back she had suffered so early in her life had retarded her and the food we gave her went into building her body and not growing feathers. In fact the process was so gradual we were hardly aware of it happening.

Then one day we came home after being out for a couple of hours and Pat, looking quickly around the kitchen floor, said,

'Where's Henrietta?' The heron was then too big to miss, unless she'd hidden herself away somewhere, which she wasn't in the habit of doing. But you never knew with birds . . .

So we hunted around, looking under the furniture and behind it, in the front room and the scullery. No heron. Then Pat thought to look up instead of down and there, standing motionless at the end of the bookcase, was Henrietta.

She'd got her wings and found she could fly. So she'd flown . . . up on top of the bookcase, where she perched like a very long-legged hawk, her head nearly touching the ceiling.

Once she'd got the hang of that she wanted to be at it all the time. A fully grown heron immobile on the settee for weeks meant little more than the minor inconvenience of having nowhere for guests to sit; the same bird skimming round the kitchen was guaranteed to make life impossible for everyone. Henrietta had to go outside to the aviary.

She settled down there straight away, even with the antisocial Perdita for company, and we had to think about finding a permanent home for her. Wherever she went, and it must be a safe place with plentiful food, she had to have her wings clipped to prevent her from flying off. Fit as she was in herself her damaged leg would always be a permanent handicap. Out in the wild, splashing clumsily through the water, she would be back where she started, with starvation slowly and inevitably overtaking her.

But before we could arrange anything we found ourselves in possession of another heron, which was extraordinary in such a short space of time, considering we had never even had one before. This was brought to us from Northwich; like Henrietta, its trouble was starvation, but this time from a different cause.

It had been found on a lake that had once been a heronry. There had been reports of herons returning there, partly from instinct (herons will return to the same site year after year), partly because there was nowhere else within range for them to go. But the lake, like so many stretches of water throughout the country once the habitat of wading birds – and so many other creatures – had become polluted by effluent, all the natural food had been destroyed and there was nothing for them to live

76

on.

This heron was in far better shape than Henrietta, completely undamaged, strong enough to stand, just very, very hungry. We fed it and put it in the aviary. From its condition it was obvious it would soon be fit enough to return to the wild, and following our policy of interfering with nature as little as possible, we didn't attempt to accustom it to any conditions that might hamper its chances when it went free.

However, there was one thing we didn't think to take into account, but within a couple of days it was brought forcibly to our notice . . .

One morning we heard a terrible din from the aviary: croaks and squawks, flailings and flappings. We rushed out and found Henrietta's long neck firmly in Perdita's claw. Perdita, the evil-tempered and possessive buzzard, had put up with one heron as company for a week, when another moved in on her it was just too much – she grabbed at the first one she could reach, and it had to be Henrietta, whose twisted leg made her so much less agile than the other heron.

It was not a case of forcibly wresting Henrietta from Perdita's grasp, as soon as I stepped into the aviary Perdita let go – she knew who was boss and, being what she was, she would really rather have people's legs than anything. Not that she dared make for mine, and Pat knew better than to get herself within range, but it was plain from the glare in Perdita's eye that it wouldn't be long before she had another taste of heron. Henrietta, ruffled and outraged, was carried out and put into the extension.

It now became a pressing matter to find a home for two herons as soon as possible and once again we approached Peter Grayson, who was able to offer room for them at the zoo. Before we could take them there coincidence – which isn't permissible in fiction and trips people up at every turn in real life – provided us with our third heron.

This, like the second bird, had come from the polluted lake. Famished, and in desperation, it had eaten anything it could find, and whatever it found was poisoned. It arrived in a deplorable state and after a quick examination we knew this was one bird that wasn't going to make it. Paradoxically, when a bird's starving it's got a chance, but when hunger overcomes it to the stage where it will eat whatever lies about it, then it could swallow all sorts of stuff and the damage already be at work in it. That was the case with this heron, before we committed ourselves to any action the decision was made for us, and it died. 'Well,' Pat said, 'three out of three is perhaps a little too much to hope for. At least the other two are all right.'

And, completely restored to health, the two herons were soon transported to the zoo. We had undertaken to get them there and the only way was by car. The herons didn't mind a bit. We carried them out, one each, lifted them into the back and placed them side by side. There they remained for the journey, staring unblinkingly through the window, standing with the utmost gravity, sleek, well-fed and elegant, like two ushers on their way to a society wedding.

The problem of pollution, of which the herons were a particular example, is a great sickness at the heart of our hygienic and technological age. More and more substances with ever more virulent side-effects are being manufactured, they have countless uses – many, I know are beneficial – but once these chemicals have served their purpose and have to be disposed of – that, all too often, is where the nightmare begins.

And it is a nightmare. Pat and I have seen some horrible sights, handled the pitiful victims of pollution, helped some but been forced to kill others to put an end to their suffering. Industry multiplies and extends, as unstoppable as the sorcerer's apprentice, and spreads with it its rubbish and toxic waste – kerosene is dumped into pools, factories clean out their boilers and storage tanks and pump the residue on to the nearest piece of waste ground. It's true there are regulations governing disposal but the regulations in themselves aren't always adequate and too little account is taken of seepage, spread, the effects of certain types of waste being exposed to the air for long periods, or coming into contact with other substances.

I know I'm sticking my neck out when I say this, but I don't think these regulations are always observed. I would like to believe – for our own well-being and the safety of our wild life – that when every load of waste leaves a factory its destination is an approved, regularly inspected area, that when it leaves and when it arrives it is logged and checked, that there are records available to state what it carried, how much, when, and what happened to it. I'd like to believe that, but I don't.

There have been times when I've tried to track down who tipped a certain type of waste, or attempted to get something moved or covered over, but always I've come up against the intricate, untraceable threads that go to make up the web of officialdom. *I'm sorry, sir, that's not our department . . . The person handling that is away on leave . . . That comes under a different authority now . . .* And so on. But there was one time when I had a go, and won – at least, I like to think I did. And it wasn't, for once, anything to do with birds.

Not far from us there is a tip and what goes into it is best not thought about. We – all of us – make rubbish in the course of our daily lives and it has to find a home *somewhere*; if it's a long way down, out of sight and covered with the regulation layer of earth each night, that's the best that can be done. In this instance, none of those requirements were met. The offending object was half a cow carcase. It was about three feet inside the iron railings that surround the tip and it obviously hadn't been thrown there from the road because the railings are too high for anyone to get it over the top; so it must have fallen off a load coming through the main gates and no one had bothered to pick it up and cart it on to the tip itself. In consequence it was only a few feet away from the road and in sight of the houses opposite – and in a very short space of time what could be seen from those houses was half the rat population of Levenshulme making for the carcase to feed on it.

Of course, the people immediately affected complained – and got nowhere. After about five days people in the neighbouring streets were also complaining as they opened their front doors and saw rats passing on their way to the tip. A lot of frustrated, frightened and horrified people had tried to get something done without any effect at all and one of them, I don't know why, came to me. I couldn't believe that any authority could allow such a state of things to go on day after day, and I went to take a look. Sure enough, there it was, a carcase grey with rats within a few feet of the pavement and no more than seventy-five yards from the nearest house.

I went home, phoned the public health department and told them the situation. I was passed from one section to the other in the leisurely manner I suspect is a technique perfected over the years for the purpose of driving anyone who complains so insane with boredom they just give up and go away. However, I stuck it out and eventually a cool voice informed me that 'the matter has been noted and will be dealt with in due course'. Due course.

'Will you,' I said, 'tell the feller who's got the matter in hand to be at that tip at ten o'clock in the morning. Because the *Guardian*, the *News of the World* and the *Manchester Evening News* will be there, too. They're coming to watch me shoot the rats.'

They weren't, of course, they didn't know a thing about it, but while I'd been hanging on the end of that line I'd had plenty of time to think something up. Anything. If you're going to tell a lie, tell a big one.

In less than an hour a team had arrived, buried the carcase and put rat poison down. I'm not to know whether it was on their work schedule already, maybe it was, although to leave the thing five days was a disgrace, anyway. They didn't half shift, though, when they finally got going.

The herons driven by hunger to feed from their poisoned pool was only one instance of what chemicals and pollution are doing to wild life. We've had birds covered in oil, birds partially or completely paralysed as a result of feeding from crops sprayed by organo-chlorine pesticides, and we had some seagulls once in a state I've never seen before and never want to see again.

They came to us in ones and twos, brought by local people who had found them lying helplessly about on the road. They were covered in a green, sticky substance, something of the texture of green soft soap. That was the nearest we could get to a

80

description of the stuff – what it really was neither of us could even guess at. Well, caked (and I must admit, disgusting) as these seagulls were we set about doing what we always did in cases of this kind, washing with a mild detergent and warm water. As we bathed the birds it became apparent that detergent simply wouldn't do. The tacky stuff spread and stuck, to our horror we found that where any of it had got under the feathers and on to the skin – the skin simply stripped off.

We scarcely had time to take in what was happening before we realised there was a further, terrible effect – the action of water caused some change in the consistency of the stuff – it began to solidify. In minutes it went rigid, encasing the birds in a grotesque, green glass. We used the ether quickly, those poor gulls were doomed whatever happened, either from the action of the stuff on their skin or from the first shower of rain.

Other birds were brought to us. On some, the flesh was already rotting and these had to be put down at once. With others, where the stuff had coated the feathers but not penetrated the skin, we tried cleaning with Fuller's earth, our regular standby. It's always a lengthy process, using that, and in this case it was completely ineffective as well, so the only thing we could do was cut the feathers away and the stuff with it. The birds we treated like this we kept for a while, they recovered and were eventually set free.

It was from one of the local kids that we discovered the source of this terrible substance. He told us that on a nearby tip there was a pool of it, deposited there by two tankers from some chemical cleaning firm. I went along to have a look. This 'pool' of sticky goo was nearer the size of a lake, thirty feet across in some places, its depth anybody's guess – I wasn't going to wade in to find out. Immediately after I'd been to look at it it was filled in, which was a mercy, although during the time it was open countless birds must have died horrible deaths.

I have heard that research is being done to find a colour that will repel birds, the object being to dye exposed toxic waste to prevent birds landing in it or feeding from it. Birds have the same five senses as human beings, but to a greater or lesser effectiveness. Touch, taste and smell are subordinate, hearing is the second major sense, sight the first; so obviously a colour, not a smell, would be a greater repellant. Birds need water – to bathe and swim in, to drink and feed from and it is in chemical waste lagoons, poisoned ponds and canals that so many of them come to grief. Something as simple and harmless as a dye to keep them away from these poisoned sources would seem to be the answer. When, I wonder, will it be found?

No one can take count of the numbers and type of wild life disappearing from our countryside; I tend to be more aware of the problems concerning birds because they're my special interest. By a paradox, certain birds of prey are on the increase closer to built-up areas: kestrels, for instance, are now more numerous per acre in these areas than they are per acre of farmland – a drive along any motorway will prove this point.

The reason for this is simple. Rats, mice, voles, vermin of all kinds are the main diet of kestrels. The widespread use of pesticides on farmland is killing off vermin, they have either disappeared altogether from some stretches of open land or are so badly infected that the kestrels, feeding off them, become themselves infected and die. Large amounts of rubbish are daily dumped beside motorways and main roads – everyone is familiar with the sight of crammed and over-flowing litter bins at lay-bys. An abundance of picnic left-overs not only attracts all numbers and types of vermin, it can keep them going for a very long time and these colonies, in their turn, provide food for kestrels and other birds of prey. I personally know of a couple of places within ten miles of the centre of Manchester where pairs of sparrow-hawks are nesting within a few feet of the main road, something unheard of at one time.

I know we all have to eat, and the farmer lives by the yield of his land, but the organo-chemical pesticides commonly in use don't just work on the vermin for which they're intended – they'll kill anything, and they do. Sometimes I'm appalled by the quite diabolical means to which a farmer must go to produce an extra pound or so per acre. If he could rely less on chemicals and more on birds of prey to keep pests down, the interlocking, interdependent chain of nature might not be, as I now believe, in danger of giving way altogether. The way things are going people will come to the stage where they will only be able to see birds of prey in private collections or as stuffed specimens.

Sometimes I remember those walks along the river bank I took as a boy and I can't help thinking that the wonder and interest of all I saw and heard then will soon be gone completely. When I take in poisoned, paralysed and rotting birds I ask myself how long it will be before this breed becomes extinct . . . then this . . . then this . . . We grow more and more civilised and in doing so make the world a marvellous place to live in — for us. But what about the emptiness when those marvels, the wild birds, are all dead?

Eight

Swans

Of all the birds that found refuge with us, none had quite the pathetic dignity of Odette, the mute female swan.

She had been seen lying on the mud bank of the Manchester Ship Canal; local people had noticed her for several days but no one approached her too closely, swans are intimidating in size and have a reputation for aggression. Eventually, when she showed no sign of moving, someone realised something must be wrong and contacted an animal welfare society which went down to the canal one bitter New Year's Eve to collect her.

Old, crippled with arthritis, she was lying in a shallow depression in the thick, oily mud. All the time she had been there she had been attempting to feed herself by stretching out her long neck and burrowing her beak in the mud in search of insects, worms, anything. After almost a week she had exhausted whatever nutriment lay within range and, exhausted herself, was starving to death.

When we took her in she was in a shocking state – thin, helpless and plastered with mud, too ill to protest against being handled or to react to the strangeness of her surroundings: the warm kitchen, the birds and cats watching her from their perches and chairs.

The first necessity, as always, was food. As Pat held the limply graceful neck I stuffed meat into the beak; by the wear round the beak I reckoned that she was an old swan, perhaps about twenty years old. We knew that if we put her outside straight away her age and condition combined would reduce her chance of survival, so – inconvenient though it was – she had to stay in the kitchen.

The inconvenience was not merely in her size. She was also filthy, and she smelled. There was nothing for it, Pat said, but to wash her . . . Some time later, saturated but persevering, she had cause to reflect on the manner in which people generally spent New Year's Eve, and the pleasures she herself had enjoyed in the past. Washing a swan – however apathetic – with a six foot wing span in a small kitchen might not be everyone's idea of celebrating a festival but in a household where anything could happen it had an entertainment value all its own.

For sheer size Odette now held the record. The cats, possibly in respect of this, kept their distance and Odette in her turn ignored them. Too ill to bother with anything, her pride turned to indifference, she lay in a collapse of snowy feathers. Pressed for room, we edged our way round her. Mindful of her despairing grace but nevertheless requiring somewhere to put her feet when she sat down, Pat gently picked up the long, outstretched neck and tucked it close to Odette's body. I watched this with interest. 'That's the first time I've seen a bird folded up.'

'Well, it doesn't do to let them get untidy, does it?' Pat said.

Odette stayed in the kitchen for two days. She paid no attention to the cats who after a decent interval prowled softly round her on their tour of inspection; at first she had been too ill to care about them, by the time her recovery began she had accepted their presence.

This aloof attitude extended to Pat, who had to pick her up and put her in different parts of the room as she went about her cleaning. A sure sign that Odette was getting better came when she growled. Pat had just moved her out of the way of the vacuum cleaner and put her down in a corner – she turned and looked at the growl with interest. It was almost a visible thing, a noise that began towards the base of the neck, travelled up it and came out of the beak as a *hiss*. Pat knew she was being warned off. She did not believe that the swan was turning aggressive – in fact she proved always to be the most docile creature – but with some sympathy Pat felt that Odette was entitled to her token protest. To be picked up and dumped here and there like an old parcel was scarcely in keeping with the dignity of such a fine lady.

Very soon Odette could stand and feed herself and was ready to go outside. We improvised a lean-to in the corner of the yard, facing the aviary, and she took up her quarters there, a majestic lodger and object of interest to anyone who called. Her first visitor was our friend Meg, dropping by to wish us happy New Year. Out in the yard, Meg went and knelt beside Odette, said 'Hallo,' and put her arms round her. 'It's the first time I've actually *held* a swan . . .' Odette just stood there, looking gracious, then unconcernedly accepted a piece of bread Meg gave her.

And most of the time she stayed with us, Odette was serenely approachable, but she did have her off days, when she was 'not at home' to callers. Then she would stand in her lean-to, looking distinctly anti-social, and set the growl off on its protracted journey up her long neck. 'Mmm, I don't think I'd bother if I were you,' Pat would say mildly to the would-be visitor.

Feeding Odette was something of a problem. She had a passion for bread but we knew this was not sufficient to sustain her. Local people constantly offered us food of amazing variety, we were always finding little parcels of bread and vegetable leaves and potato peelings shoved in a corner of the porch, so one day when an acquaintance of Pat's, who ran a local children's nursery, asked if the left-overs from the nursery dinners would be of any use, Pat said yes, of course. She was prepared to try anything on the ever-expanding army of dependents who looked to her for food every day.

She received a bucket of what she could only term 'indescribably revolting *stuff*' and took it out and plonked it in the yard. Odette, who was wandering about looking dignified, immediately made for the bucket and put her head in it. Pat studied her wryly, thinking to herself how she was going to have to sort the stuff out, somehow, and expecting Odette to draw back in aristocratic horror.

Odette, however, had found an alternative to bread – or, in view of the miscellaneous contents of the bucket – several alternatives. From that day onwards, Odette's feeding problem was solved. It didn't matter to her what was in the bucket – cottage pie and jelly, bubble and squeak and custard – if, before she started they were not all mixed together to a state that would have made the strongest stomach curdle, they were by the time she was halfway through. It was her party, and she adored it; she certainly thrived on it. But she wouldn't give up entirely her first passion – bread. Every evening, before she settled down for the night, she would delicately stretch out her long neck and accept a slice of bread from Pat; holding it in her beak, she'd slosh it about in the bowl of water always at her side, soaking it until it was soft, then consuming it contentedly. A nice, plain supper to round off the gastronomic delights of the day.

She couldn't stay in the yard forever. She grew fit, although still to a degree afflicted by arthritis – a condition which, in view of her age, would never improve. Her slow, creaking gait prompted us to refer to her as 'the little old lady'. But, creaking or not, she needed a great deal of room to move and a fair stretch of water as well, so we had to find a home for her.

Eventually, we did – a little hill-top farm in Derbyshire with sympathetic owners and ideal conditions and one Sunday morning we took her there. Pat and I were in the front of the car and Odette, regal and unruffled, sat on the back seat. We set out at five thirty, just as it was light and the roads were free of traffic, and on the journey encountered only one motorist – possibly a late-night reveller returning home – who almost went through his windscreen at the incredible spectacle of a swan being taken for a drive.

For a while we kept in touch with her new owners to check up on how she was getting on. 'How is Odette getting on? Oh, fine . . . one way and another.'

What *did* that mean? Well, it seemed that, perfect as her surroundings were she nevertheless, after a short time, took it into her head to do some exploring. One sleepy summer afternoon when no one was inclined to notice anything much, she left the farm and set off walking down the hill to the village. Unafraid, indeed with a majestic lack of regard for the consternation of the shoppers in the high street, she creaked along, the little old lady enjoying a pleasant stroll. Someone who spotted her knew where she was from and told the police, who temporarily took charge of her while phoning the owners to come and collect her.

Undeterred, Odette later made a second journey, then a third . . . In time she became a familiar sight in the village, wandering along the street to her inevitable destination – the police station. For a swan that had ridden in cars and had a bath in a kitchen, being taken in charge really meant nothing at all.

Our first contact with Belle Vue zoo was made when we needed advice about feeding Henrietta; then, as I related, Peter Grayson offered the two herons a home. When we took them there they went to live in a large enclosure with the Sarus cranes and crowned cranes, a showy contrast to their sober grey and white. The enclosure had a high wire fence round it but was open at the top. Of the two herons only Henrietta had her wings clipped, the other was left just as it was and after a couple of weeks it took itself off and returned to the wild.

We began calling in at the zoo at weekends, first to take a look at the herons and see how they were going on, then just to potter around. The pottering became a habit. It was natural that when occasion arose we'd make ourselves useful, cleaning up, helping to get food ready, washing out bowls – anything to lend a hand, and the daily life of a zoo is fascinating to anyone interested in birds and animals. Our over-crowding problem at home arose as a matter of course; Peter thought it would be a good idea to have some of our kestrels at the zoo for people to see and he put a cage at our disposal.

It was in the Pheasantries, a very large, airy cage overhung by willows at the end of a walk bordered by shrubs. We seemed to fill it in no time, and various owls we had too little room for at home began to move in with the kestrels. It soon became apparent that our strays needed yet more room, so Peter and I looked around and found that the children's zoo provided the answer. There were two big semi-circular cages there, looking out at the pond and the Noah's ark and the miniature train; the kestrels went in one cage and the owls in another. Generally they were birds that were recovering from some kind of injury or orphans that had to learn to fend for themselves in company with others;

most of them in time made a full recovery and were released.

In the main part of the zoo was a delightful pond, called the Square pond. It was a paved area set inside a low wall and planted with sycamores, elms and flowering cherry and tall willows that dipped and trailed in the water. Shallow steps went down into the pond and there was an island with a four section shelter, this was where the waterfowl could nest if they wanted to, and sometimes breed. From time to time several of our ducks and geese went to join the waterfowl already there.

So, with keeping an eye on our birds and generally lending a hand, we became regular fixtures at the zoo. When a staff problem came up Pat, knowing the routine, offered to stand in if it would help. Before she knew what had happened she had got herself a job one day a week, then somehow the one became two. Her principal work was in the preparation of food. She didn't in the least mind acting as canteen lady to a lot of animals, it was just like home, really, only bigger.

In about the coldest week of the winter we had a call from the RSPCA in the Walkden area to say they were bringing two swans to us, one of them injured. There's a stretch of open land that was once mining country and after the pits fell into disuse they were flooded and fenced. The lakes that were formed are called lodges, they go down the hillsides in a series of levels. It's a bleak enough spot at the best of times and in mid-winter it's enough to chill the blood. I was glad we didn't have to go out there ourselves.

Swans are a common sight around there, they've been breeding on the lodges for many years. It seemed that a pair of swans had taken off from one of the higher levels to fly to a lower lodge and one swan, misjudging the distance for some reason, had flown into a fence and injured itself. Someone had seen it hanging around all day, trying to move occasionally but most of the time just sitting.

They reported this to the RSPCA who went up there and picked up the swan without any trouble. It was a male and its mate, not injured herself, had stayed beside it. Swans are faithful birds and when they pair it's generally for life. Knowing this, and not wishing to separate them, the RSPCA men netted the female and brought her along to us as well.

When they arrived it was fairly late at night. We'd been pretty crowded the time we had Odette but two fully grown swans and four adults would have gone a fair way to making our kitchen unbearable. Fortunately the RSPCA men had to dash off on another job and couldn't stay. They passed the swans over to us virtually on the doorstep, with what information they had about the male – 'There's some damage to its wing, possibly elsewhere as well because it doesn't seem to be able to move at all . . .'

We carried them into the kitchen, a swan apiece, and put them down, side by side, in front of the fire. From armchairs and settee the cats, mildly put out, viewed them, yawned and settled back with a feline resignation that seemed to say there had to be a limit to what would fit in our kitchen . . . surely this was it?

I examined the male swan and found some bruising under one wing and on the shoulder, but there didn't seem to be anything more serious than that, no broken bones or wounds. It hissed a bit, and its mate hissed as well, more as a token protest than anything else. Pat and I concluded the male's immobility was probably the result of shock. 'We'll wait a bit and see, Trish,' I said. 'Put the kettle on and we'll have a cuppa and sit with it for a while.'

We didn't have long to wait. Enough time had elapsed since its accident for the swan to go through a natural process of recovery from shock. It had a really good look round from its sitting position and after a while it got up and, joined by its mate, started to do a little exploring.

The cats had the same idea. I suppose what with the gentle Odette and the odd heron or two they were a trifle blasé about large birds. These two were a different proposition. They were healthy wild swans confined in strange surroundings for incomprehensible reasons and they didn't go much on cats at all. In no time they were making this clear, barging about and clouting with their beaks whatever bottom came within reach. There were hisses and yowls, the air was full of darting white necks

91

and hurtling Siamese cats, spilt cups of coffee and Pat and I diving to the rescue.

We shoo'd the swans together and got them into the extension. This was an extra room I'd built just outside the scullery, in a corner formed by the yard and the wall of the house. I sometimes think I've spent half my life looking for space to *put things* the way other men devote themselves to prospecting for gold. Injured birds stayed close to us, where we could keep an eye on them, those that were well on the mend to the point where they could hang on to their own food and generally look after themselves lived in the outdoor aviary. But there were the halfway cases and the problem of where to put them where they wouldn't be under our feet and at the same time not in danger of being lost amongst the other birds if anything went wrong.

So I built the extension. All sorts of tackle found its way in there, as well as the birds that could be called 'walking wounded' – seagulls recovering from smashed wings, as a rule, who needed room away from the other birds and quiet until they began to fly again. Just by good luck it was at that time unoccupied, although as it is half the size of the kitchen it could scarcely be said to be roomy accommodation. However, it had to do for the night and some degree of tranquillity had to be maintained. We gave the swans some bread and wheat and they fell to eating at once with the wonderful disdain of royal creatures who don't give a hang for the havoc they leave in their wake.

First thing in the morning I phoned Peter at Belle Vue and told him we had two swans to dispose of in a hurry – the ideal place to do it was the lake at the zoo. He said yes, of course, so after breakfast I had a quick look at the male swan – it was, as I'd anticipated, perfectly all right. We carried the swans out, put them in the back of the car and drove to Belle Vue.

The lake there, which in the summer months is used as a boating lake, is very large and we could drive right to the edge of it. Peter was there waiting for us. The weather was absolutely bitter and wrapped up as we were, we were nevertheless pinched with cold in no time as we stood and had a consultation.

We'd thought of the lake as it was the nearest stretch of water

A magpie, heron, crow, kestrel, goose and two owls in part of the backyard aviary

Bob with Medusa, a male buzzard with a broken leg

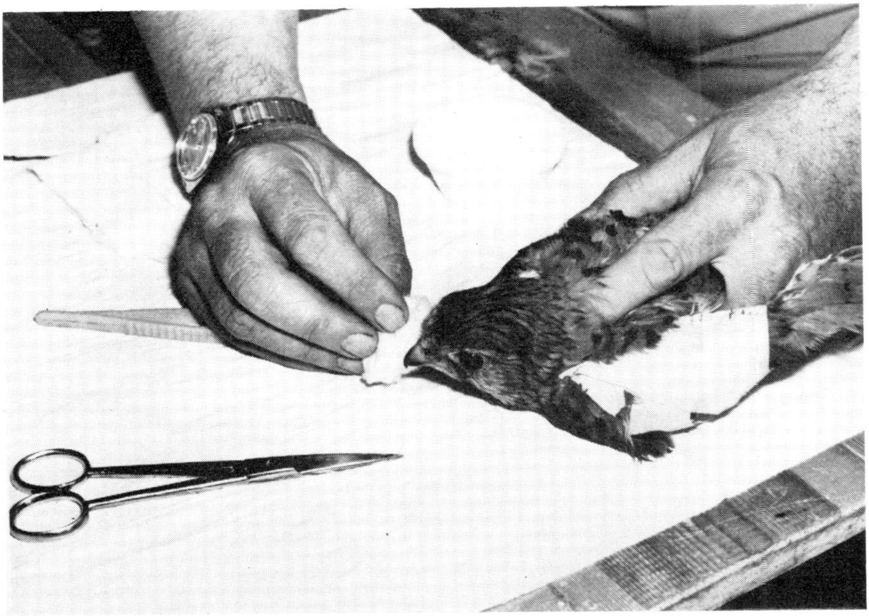

Bob tending a kestrel with a broken wing

Nine kestrels and an owl in the aviary

of any reasonable size and safe, clean and quiet; swans need plenty of space to get themselves airborne. As we stood there and talked about it we decided that as there was a good wind blowing in the right direction there was every possibility we could launch the swans and get them airborne straight away, without having to put them on the water. We've done this before with big birds. If the conditions are favourable they lift up like sail planes and are off without the slightest trouble – but there's always the water there, in case they don't make it.

When I say the wind was in the right direction what I mean is that it was blowing straight across from Siberia with enough force to bleach your bones. At least, that's what it felt like. I took the male swan from the car, carried it to the edge of the lake, raised it above my head and launched it. Pat, meanwhile, did the same with the other swan.

There were two consecutive flops and down they both went, sending great showers of icy water all over us. It seemed they just weren't in the mood for getting into the air that way.

Never mind, we said, attempting to dry ourselves off, they just want to have a swim round for a while and then they'll go. So we waited, stamping our feet and hugging into our coats, gradually getting more and more frozen. The swans sailed about and began feeding. There was plenty in the way of sticklebacks and crustacea in the lake, enough to keep them happy for a long while, and they seemed perfectly content.

After an hour had gone by they showed no signs of leaving, but we had to, before we perished from exposure. And it was just as well we didn't wait for their actual take-off . . . They stayed three days before flying away.

Another swan that took its time about getting airborne was one that we didn't actually deal with ourselves, although I'd like to have been there to see it.

Just after eight o'clock one morning Pat had a phone call from the police in Bramhall and they asked for me. Pat said I had gone off to work – could she help?

'Well, it's a bit awkward. It's a swan, you see, it's come down on the main road.'

'Is it hurt?' Pat asked.

No, she was assured, it wasn't hurt, it had just landed and was – sort of – walking about.

'In the main road?' Pat said. She looked at the clock, it was just about the time everyone was driving to work. 'Isn't it causing a bit of a disturbance?'

'Well, yes, it is rather. It's quite safe at the moment, we've got the traffic down to single line and we're directing it round it. Er – it's just sort of walking backwards and forwards, though, and we're not quite sure what it'll do next. So there's a policeman accompanying it.'

'I see . . .' Pat said, trying not to laugh at the sudden mental picture of the unlikely pair patrolling a busy road while commuters sat behind the wheels of their cars, fuming. 'I'm afraid I can't do anything, but I'll give you my husband's number.'

I got the phone call, and the story, within minutes. 'Keep it there,' I said – not really thinking, it was just a matter of habit, I suppose, to say a thing like that. 'And give me half an hour to get myself organised and I'll be over to collect it.'

Just as I was about to leave there was another call, the same police inspector again. 'Not to worry, it's gone.'

I asked had somebody been along to pick it up and after a moment's strained silence the inspector answered, 'No, it went of its own accord, Mr Ratcliffe. The bloody thing ran two hundred yards up the main road looking like a jumbo jet with the wings flapping. The man I had accompanying it kept pace – you had, after all, instructed us to keep it here. Mindful of this, I'm sure, my man decided he ought to – er – detain it. Unfortunately, just as he made a grab for it, it took off, and he went headlong . . .'

Yes, I'd like to have been there to see that.

Nine

Learning to fly

At that time, in addition to the birds, there were two hedgehogs resident in the aviary. The first one had been acquired after it had accidentally been dug up by a ferret. The man who owned the ferret knew it would do no good to put the hedgehog back after its hibernation had been broken, instead he took it home and fed it. Later in the day he came round to us and handed it over, saying he was sure Pat would like it –

'And tell her not to bother about its supper today. I've given it plenty of bread and milk.'

'I wish he *hadn't*,' Pat said feelingly, after he'd gone. He meant well, of course, but she'd had hedgehogs before and remembered only too well the effect of bread and milk on their systems. She spent the rest of the evening and half the night mopping up after it.

The weather was still far too cold for it to go outdoors straight away and it needed to adapt its system to waking several weeks too early. It also needed to develop its feeding routine. Pat saw that it got the correct diet and, as she was going to be stuck with it indoors for a while, she housetrained it.

The cats' litter boxes were in the extension I'd built opening onto the scullery, and it seemed only sensible to Pat to put one out there for the hedgehog, too. He learned to use it in an amazingly short time (she kept quiet about her methods, – I think she just used to threaten him with unspeakable things when no one was around to hear); he'd scamper out when necessary and then back again to his temporary home, a box in an alcove under the bookcase.

Slightly cantakerous and self-contained, he kept to his nocturnal habits, sleeping during the day and in the night getting up to potter about. In the silence and stillness of the house, after everyone else had retired, we'd hear him noisily gobbling up any dinner the cats had left uneaten. As soon as possible he went into the aviary and after a while there was joined by the second hedgehog.

This was one we'd found wandering about in the road one night. 'It'll only get itself run over,' Pat said. 'Besides, it can keep the other one company.' So we took it back with us and put it in the aviary, where it made its home with the other one, not at all bothered by the birds, who don't bother with them – even the owls respect their prickles. Great scavengers, the hedgehogs emerge at night to eat every scrap they can find, effectively cleaning the aviary from dusk till dawn, when they go back to bed to sleep off their labours.

The hedgehogs were about the only creatures that needed no attention of any kind. Everything else had to be fed and cared for in some way, and one of Pat's never-ending jobs was keeping the house in a respectable condition, and Jeannie was forever under her feet.

The fishing hawk was a ground dweller. I guessed that she had been taken straight from her nest and never flown, as she certainly seemed to have no idea what her wings were for. So she spent most of her time on the floor, walking and hopping about; when Pat put her on the back of the settee, or a chair, she simply stayed there. If she was left too long she grew bored and began her absurd squeaking, asking to be taken down and put somewhere else.

Her fits became less and less frequent until, thankfully, they stopped altogether, although she still needed to be kept on her vitamin diet; and her feathers began to grow.

They didn't grow very well. The near starvation of her early life had left its legacy in hunger traces – the same weakening condition that had affected Kit, although with him it was only the tail, with Jeannie it was all over. On the finer feathers the hunger traces, although present, were not too obvious, but on the heavier primaries and secondaries they showed up as bars, as many as four or five to each feather. Any exertion on her part and the new feathers snapped. It soon became apparent that they would never be strong enough to allow her much flight; sooner or later she would attempt to fly, but until that time came she was quite happy on two legs, keeping company with the cats.

Tan, the eldest Siamese, had died, but the sadness his death caused was soon softened by the arrival of another, a lilac Siamese called Dinah. She was a stray, under sentence of death if no home could be found for her. Someone offered her to us and we didn't think twice about accepting. Within a short time of her arrival she presented us with a surprise litter of five coal black kittens — evidence of the indiscriminate way she had spent her time when she was homeless.

Jeannie was fascinated by the kittens. From a safe distance she would stand and stare at them gathered around Dinah, a mass of tiny bodies, tangled and fumbling. When they began to find their feet and stagger about she watched their progress with interest. Eventually, an adventurous one, lurching at high speed, lost its balance and tumbled against her long legs. She let out a screech, drawing her body up tall and thin in amazement. Standing absolutely still, with the kitten gambolling round her feet, she began her silly, plaintive squeak as if to communicate her outrage to Pat — 'It *touched* me!' — 'Well, if you will stay on the floor instead of learning to fly, what do you expect?' Pat said to her.

Jeannie soon got over her shock. The first kitten was followed by a second, the second by a third. A game developed in which all five would chase her, patting at her newly sprouting tail feathers with their paws; when she'd had enough she'd turn round and rush at them, herding them all back to Dinah.

Because the floor was getting too crowded, or because she wanted a little peace, or simply because it was time, Jeannie began to try her wings. I've kept so many birds from nestlings and watched them learn to fly, but I've never known the process take so long. Possibly Jeannie's long, severe illness retarded her development and her early treatment had dislocated some sense of co-ordination. Clutching at the back of a chair she would flap her wings, hesitantly at first, almost as if she expected them to fall off, then more and more violently, getting nowhere in a tremendous pother, finally giving up in a collapse of effort, faintly puzzled to find herself in exactly the same place.

She tried this many times, and the noise could be heard all over the house. Pat, listening, would think to herself: *there she goes again* . . . Sometimes she went to watch the performance, saying encouragingly, 'Fly, you fool.' But this was altogether taking things too fast for Jeannie.

Finally, in a moment of extreme daring, after beating the air for minutes on end, Jeannie pitched herself forward. The split second she was suspended in space astonished her so much she completely forgot what she was about, shut her wings and crashed down on the seat of the chair. She was extremely put out about this, but it didn't stop her doing it again – and again – and again. The original sound of her threshing wings was replaced by the sound of her body landing on chairs all over the place.

After a while she tried a variation. She began on the floor, taking absurd little sprints that terminated in a mad, vaulting leap. Wings working violently, she kept herself airborne for a few seconds, her long legs trailing, an expression on her face that might have said, 'What am I *doing*?' Whatever it was, it unnerved her. She stopped using her wings and grabbed for the floor and, her balance completely gone, finished in an undignified heap.

As time went by she *had* to get the hang of it, and eventually she did, extremely inefficiently, and she was a very big bird to be doing gymnastics about the place. She knew when her meal-times were, but the mealtimes of human beings meant nothing to her. More than once she launched herself from the back of the sofa on to the kitchen table. If I didn't whip my plate out of the way quickly enough she landed in it. Too concerned with herself to care about my resigned, 'That's my *dinner* . . .' she'd pick herself up, walk across the table and fling herself off from the other side of it.

98

With her plumage growing her bulk increased and she was more and more in Pat's way. She even began to follow her upstairs, leaping from step to step as the stairs were much too narrow for her to spread her wings and fly. Once or twice she attempted to come down, half tumbling, half hauling herself with a weird rowing action, landing at the bottom dishevelled and fed-up. She soon gave up trying altogether, and it was the realisation that Jeannie could get up and not down that gave Pat the idea of putting her in the bedroom during the times there was work to be done and her presence would be a nuisance.

As soon as the bed was made in the morning, Pat would cover it with newspaper. Jeannie liked to perch on the bed-head, which was against the window, and look down into the street. Or she could practise her flying, on to the wardrobe and back, on to the top of the door and round to the wardrobe again. Pat always left the door open; flying to and from it Jeannie closed it till there was no more than a gap. When she was bored with her own company and wanted some attention, Jeannie perched on the door, twisting herself down and round so that she could peep through the gap. Every so often, just to remind Pat she was there, she would give her silly squeak.

But she wasn't completely alone. Boo, being so much smaller, could manage the narrow stairs without any trouble. In the mornings he would find his way up and in through the open door, and all the time Jeannie was there he stayed, too, flying about, peering from the window, sharing the top of the door, squabbling occasionally.

Pat, hearing Jeannie's insistent aren't-you-coming-to-take-me-downstairs squeak, would look up and see two heads, a large and a small, peeping through the gap of the almost closed door. Two birds might have seemed enough in one bedroom; but there was plenty of space, and Pat did not mind who kept Jeannie company so long as they kept her quiet. There was room for one more . . .

One day a rational, reasoning human being took a female kestrel, tied its wings and feet together, wrapped it tightly with wire and put it in the road.

Why?

To anyone asking this question I can only give a shrug of the shoulders and a comprehensive expression of disgust. Viciousness towards helpless creatures is something I've experienced time and again, the ability to explain it is beyond me – as it is beyond most people. Somewhere, at any given moment, some creature is suffering needlessly, senselessly, wastefully. Seeing so much evidence of this, I have had to come to terms with the reality of it, just as I have had to come to terms with my own helplessness to prevent it. All I can do is give help when asked.

The kestrel was brought to me by a stranger who had stopped his car by chance and looked out of the window and seen her lying in the gutter. Although badly knocked about, she had no broken bones; she was extremely dejected, though, very undernourished and very frightened. I gave her a good feed as soon as she arrived and – seeing she was fully grown and quite wild, put her in the outside aviary at once in the hope that when she recovered I would be able to release her.

The original aviary had been extended bit by bit until it took up almost the whole of the yard. Part of it was under cover, and in that part were branches, perches, nesting boxes; in the outer area there were more perches and small receptacles for use as baths. The birds lived there happily, in conditions as near natural as possible, adapting themselves to changes in the weather as they would have done in the wild. Most of them were permanently injured in some way and would never fly free again.

One resident who would not be staying beyond the time he had learned to fend for himself was a very young kestrel, another survivor of the senseless urge to destroy.

Some time previously there had been a spate of window-breaking at a local mill. No one could account for this at first until someone who worked there discovered it was boys throwing stones, not indiscriminately, but because they were aiming at something specific. The broken windows were incidental, the real target was a nest of birds on the roof.

A young employee of the mill went up to investigate and discovered three nestlings: one dead, two just alive – the mother bird having finally been frightened off, perhaps killed, by the

100

stones. He brought the two youngsters down and handed them in at his nearest RSPCA branch, who passed them over to me. Pip and Squeak, tiny creatures with down like day-old chicks, and needle sharp beaks and claws, lived in a box in the kitchen for a while, too young to be frightened and not interested in anything except food. When they began to get adventurous they were put up on the sideboard, out of the way of feet, and they made their home there amongst the ornaments and books, pottering about, peering down at the floor below and up at the kestrels who flew about the room.

From this vantage point they went through the clownish performance of learning to fly: elevating themselves by a frantic flapping of wings and bouncing down in surprise when they realised they were airborne. In fits of daring they would scamper along the sideboard and keep going when they'd run out of anything to scamper on, flailing away to prevent a too rapid descent, struggling to find their impulsion with a desperate air that seemed to say: If I keep doing this I'm *bound* to fly . . .

When they were really getting the hang of taking care of themselves they went outside to the aviary. I looked forward to releasing the pair together but one day I found Squeak dead. I could discover no reason for the young kestrel's death, it was just something that had happened, and that was that. Pip was left to wait his time for freedom alone.

One day during a very cold spell we went out to the aviary to clean it and feed the birds. In the quiet of the morning a peculiarly persistent wheezing noise sounded very loud. It wasn't the wheezing that was unfamiliar to Pat, only its unexpectedness. She looked at me. 'Are you having one of your asthmatic turns?'

I shook my head. For years I've been subject to such attacks – not that morning, though. 'No, I'm perfectly all right,' I answered. 'But someone isn't.'

We searched amongst the birds and eventually, tracking the noise to its source, discovered the culprit to be the latest female, the one that had been found wrapped in wire. As she fluttered about the wheezing became louder and soon an obvious breathlessness forced her to be still. As I picked her up I realised that this was very probably how someone had managed to catch her in the first place; too much exertion simply exhausted her, once she had flown herself out of breath she was helpless.

I took her indoors and treated her to a simple, age-old remedy: peppercorns. These cured her bad chest and when the weather was a little milder I tried her outside once more. Soon, she was at it again, wheezing away. It seemed that the slightest change in temperature affected her.

I brought her in and treated her again. The more I handled her and kept her indoors the more difficult it would be for her to return to wild conditions; also, it soon became apparent that her chances were far from good – with her weakness for catching chills and the breathlessness that would overcome her when she tried to pursue her prey. We decided she would have to stay with us and it might as well be in the house where it was warm and there was plenty of room for her to fly around. She was really quite an elderly bird and I didn't think she would have very long to live.

We called her Dianthus, shortened to Dip. She never became completely tame the way Boo did, or positively affectionate the way Jeannie was, but she was a gentle, quiet bird. Adventurous, too, once she had got her bearings, exploring in her sedate way and landing up one day in the bedroom, where she moved in with Jeannie and Boo.

Whenever we went up to her – to talk to her or to feed her – she always regarded us with docility; but after a while an odd change came over her, when I approached she would challenge me, putting her head down and scolding and mantling her plumage.

'Have you noticed anything strange about Dip lately?' I asked Pat.

Pat said she had. 'She's acting very funny, especially when you go near the wardrobe. But she's an old lady, and perhaps the others are upsetting her. You know what a bully Boo can be, and Jeannie's such a fool, barging about all over the place.'

Still, Dip didn't have to stay in the bedroom; if the others were making life uncomfortable for her there – and that was what, possibly, was happening – she was free to leave and go and live somewhere else in the house. But she stayed on top of the wardrobe.

Her behaviour even seemed to communicate itself to Boo, who was occasionally very aggresive; then one day I saw him attempting to mate with Dip. Even if it was funny it was also pathetic – the force of the instinct that drove the crippled tiercel and the elderly female to act out unavailingly the roles nature had designed for them.

Regularly, Pat had to hunt every corner of the house, not only to clean up droppings but to find any bits of meat the birds might have put away and forgotten to go back and eat. She also retrieved an assortment of objects the kestrels picked up and put somewhere else. Matches, pieces of string, cocktail sticks, hair rollers – anything light and carriable, the kestrels, or Jeannie, carried it. The top of the wardrobe was a marvellous hiding place for treasure and one of Pat's permanent jobs was standing on a chair, clearing it of clutter.

She went to do this one day, ignoring the extraordinary way that Dip, disturbed, leapt forward and challenged her.

'It's only *me* . . .' she said resignedly, reaching to lift away a canvas holdall that was kept on top of the wardrobe. But she didn't move it; she stood still for some time looking at it, then she looked at Dip.

The unaccountable behaviour was accounted for at last. The old lady was sitting on two eggs.

'What shall we do?' Pat asked me.

'Leave them,' I said. 'It's all we can do. And I'm afraid there's not much chance of them hatching, you know. Not with Jeannie around . . .'

I was right. The wardrobe, after all, was Jeannie's place, too – if anything, she had first claim on it. She made for it one day, unsettling Dip, who got off her eggs. Big, amiable, clumsy, Jeannie landed on them, and broke them.

103

Ten

Tich, a small diversion

After working at tool making for some time I moved to heavy engineering to gain more experience, then became Training Officer at the factory where I had been for some time. One day at work I got a panic-stricken request to go across to the administrative block and deal with a rat under the floorboards.

In the office two girls, close to hysteria, clutched each other and stammered about a scratching sound – 'It's trying to get *out* . . . over *there* . . .' I went to the corner they indicated and listened. It was true enough – there was an odd, faint, persistent scrabbling noise coming from somewhere.

I moved furniture, lifted the floor covering and began to prise up the boards. By then I had assistance, as some more men from the firm had arrived. They stood round, armed with various implements, poised to strike at the maddened, trapped rat when it emerged. The girls fled.

But when the boards were removed, nothing leapt out. I peered down and saw I had opened a hole directly above a drainage pit into which a pipe ran. At the bottom of the pit was something black, ceaselessly moving, scarcely four inches long. I put in my hand and took it out.

It was a kitten. Blind, helpless, its cord still wet, it could not have been more than a few hours old.

Its mother must have been the half wild female cat who prowled the outbuildings, a tiny, scrawny creature who had kittens with monotonous frequency; she had them all over the place and they were always black. It would seem, although no one could be certain, that she had crawled along the pipe into the drainage pit, given birth to this one, then crawled out again, abandoning it. If she had any others, or where she had them, we never discovered.

It was a wonder this one had not died. I saw that it very soon would, unless someone did something for it. I love cats – even if I hadn't my instinct is to save anything with life in it – so I didn't think of anything else. I wrapped it up, forced a few drops of sugar and water into its mouth, ran out to my car and drove home.

Pat was out shopping. Comfortable and warm, Dinah lay before the fire, her five kittens tumbling about round her. I unwrapped the tiny, just living scrap of a creature, put it into the heap of kittens and proceeded to mix them all up together, rubbing them against each other and over the newcomer. Then I scooped them all up and put them under Dinah.

I watched her . . . I swear she counted her five, did a double-take on the sixth, then gave the feline equivalent of a shrug, as if to say, 'Six? Oh well . . . why not?'

Naturally enough, the new kitten was called Tich, a name which later turned out to be ludicrously unsuitable. But right from the start he'd proved himself indestructible and continued in the same manner, fighting for his food with kittens several weeks old. On the day I had to take Dinah to the vet to be neutered, Tich was just over a week old; the other kittens could fend for themselves by then but Pat had to see to it that during Dinah's absence Tich was fed.

She had a preparation of rearing milk and she got it into him by using a hypodermic syringe. That sounds a bit drastic, as if she injected it, but it wasn't like that. What she did was to remove the needle and in its place fit a bicycle valve rubber, then she filled the syringe, put the rubber in Tich's mouth and pushed down the plunger, squeezing the milk into Tich. And most of the time she laughed.

Tich was so ugly, his face as flat as a pancake, with a little tube of a body from which the stumps of his legs stuck out, and a completely hairless stomach. She literally pumped him up with the syringe, watching his little bald tummy get rounder and rounder; when the milk started oozing back out of his mouth

106

she judged he'd had enough. She'd put him down next to a hot water bottle where, after a preliminary burp, he'd sink into a sleep of ecstatic repletion, packed tight as a black pudding.

We kept Dinah's kittens for eleven weeks and, like the birds, they had the run of the house. That meant that as soon as they were mobile enough they ventured upstairs, and found the bed. Our cats have always had the run of the house and, being cats, known where it's warmest and most comfortable. At night time there was quite a procession on the stairs.

One night Pat, struggling to get into bed, found that wherever she tried to put down a hand or a foot, someone had got there first. Even her patience has a limit. Pushing cats and kittens out of the way, wrestling for a place in her own bed, she said to me, 'This *cannot* go on.'

'I suppose not,' I agreed, assisting her by grabbing small furry bodies and putting them somewhere else. Anywhere. 'All right, we'll find homes for them.'

'All six.'

'All six,' I repeated, holding up the minute, ridiculous Tich.

'Well . . . five then,' Pat said.

And once Dinah's kittens were out of the way it seemed that Tich had only been waiting for space to expand. He began to grow, alarmingly, unstoppably, until he was the size of the two Siamese cats put together. Watching the transformation of the morsel of skin and fur into a great, handsome cat, I was sometimes remotely visited by the mad suspicion that Tich intended to take over the world . . .

After many years of invalidism, Pat's father died. When a bereavement occurs those who were closest take time to assimilate the new situation, that's the way it is with everyone, I imagine: things are suddenly very different and yet, on another level, they go on being just the same. After we'd sorted ourselves out we decided to take over the empty house next door, where Pat had been born and where we'd lived when we were first married.

As I've said, my life seems to be a continuous quest for space;

107

our dream is one day to have a place with ground around it where we can keep our birds and look out on fields and Pat can have a garden. Well, one day, who knows? Meanwhile, we live with things as they are and the immediate answer to our over-crowding lay to hand: by taking over Pat's father's house we could knock it together with our own.

We weren't going in for anything ambitious, it was just a matter of knocking through the kitchen wall to the left of our fireplace, thus making an opening into the corresponding kitchen in the next house. We got a friend in to do the job and as I had to be out at work all day and couldn't lend a hand, Pat had to stand in as 'mate' whenever necessary.

Modest as our project was, it caused chaos, as interior alter-ations have a way of doing, and it seemed to go on forever. Amidst the wrenchings, bangings and crashes there were squawks of protest from our various livestock and Pat was forever diving to grab something that became too inquisitive and got in the way. Clouds of brickdust rose, settled . . . and crept . . . We had brick-dust covered birds and cats and we grew resigned to the new seasoning at mealtimes: brickdust and chips, bread and butter and brickdust, custard and brick-dust . . .

But at last it was finished, and with the carpets down again and the walls papered and the furniture back in place – there still wasn't enough room. This, I think, is Parkinson's Law – something to do with things expanding to take up the space available; there is also a variation – which I modestly term Ratcliffe's first principle – which states that *birds* expand to take up the space available.

And animals, and people. We have an endless stream of visitors to the house, friends and strangers. People will come for the first time with a bird, then call again to see how it's getting on – and bring their friends with them. Entire families who've heard of us somewhere or other will knock on the door and ask if they can look at the birds. Everyone who has time and is interested is shown round. Often our kitchen is so crowded it resembles the waiting room of a very busy station.

108

One nice lady who called once told us about the bird sanctuary she ran, very much on the same lines as ours, at home. 'Where's that?' Pat asked. 'Oh, Australia,' the lady answered. Some time after that – not from the same source, from a different part of Australia – we received a letter addressed

The Man and Bird Woman
Manchester
England.

That was all it said on the envelope, but it found us.

We have phone calls from people saying they've found an injured kestrel, or an owl with a broken wing. I take the message, or Pat does, and tell them to come round – but sometimes we forget to tell each other, either there's too much to do, or a crisis occurs and our attention is taken up elsewhere. Then in the evening there'll be a knock on the door and I'll go and answer it and see a stranger, perhaps two, hovering uncertainly in the dark, clutching a box or a bundle. 'Er – Mr Ratcliffe – '

Something stirs in my memory, a half-remembered message, a scribbled note on a scrap of paper. 'Yes, I'm Bob Ratcliffe. Are you the owl?'

'No – No – ' A startled response. People unaccustomed to our verbal shorthand often seem to find it alarming. Wordlessly, the bundle – whatever it is – is proffered. Pat appears in the kitchen doorway, an ear-splitting shriek from some birds she's just abandoned accompanies her. 'No, Bob,' she said mildly, 'They'll be the kestrel who rang up this morning . . .'

'Er – no. We found these fledgelings, you see, and asked you if you – '

'Oh, yes, you'll be the two blackbirds, in need of a good feed, no doubt. Come on in and we'll take a look at you . . .'

If anyone ever flees off into the night in search of sanity, I suppose I ought not to be surprised.

With so much to occupy us we're not only absent-minded with each other, we quite often forget to mention things to our visitors as well. When we've had a clutch of ducklings floating in the bath for a few days we're so accustomed to their presence it doesn't occur to us to draw anyone's attention to them. And when a friend who was spending the afternoon with us returned from a traumatic visit to the loo – saying he'd been attacked by five baby owls – we could only offer our apologies. It had quite simply slipped my mind they were there, or I thought Pat had warned him . . .

One evening our friend Meg called to introduce her fiancé to us; we hadn't seen each other for ages and at once became immersed in catching up on our news. We're so used to silent creatures moving inquisitively about we don't even notice them any more; but as we chattered on Percy, Meg's fiancé, said less and less and grew very still, feeling himself riveted by an un-blinking face. Cautiously, he turned his head and looked down at the side of his armchair into a pair of enormous, accusing eyes.

An old owl had been having forty winks in the other kitchen until our talk disturbed it. It had walked through to find the nearest person to glare at; its hunched body and fed-up ex-pression indicated only too plainly that a chap had a devil of a job getting a bit of peace around here . . . Good God, it wasn't much to ask, was it? Having made its complaint and succeeded – temporarily at least – in silencing one voice it turned round and went noiselessly back the way it had come.

This owl had been found by some men in the workshop at a local engineering firm. He had been in some diesel oil and was exhausted and in a bit of a mess. The men had no idea what to do for him, so they phoned the police who suggested they bring him along to us. One of the firm's vans was brought out, the owl put carefully in a box and in due time an anxious deputation arrived on our doorstep, asking if we would be kind enough to do something. Owls are pretty rare in workshops and the men had taken him to their hearts.

We cleaned the owl up and kept him indoors for a while so that we could watch how he was going on. Birds don't generally show their age, but owls do; this old gentleman had lived a long time and was getting to the end of his span. When we were sure there was no other damage and nothing more we could do for him we put him in the outside aviary to end his days in peace and safety; his sharpness and agility had gone, he would have been very hard put to it to hunt, but there he had plenty. And he wasn't forgotten. After we'd had him a while we received a letter and a few pounds; the men in the workshop had had a whip round to help towards his keep – an act of uncommon consideration and, we thought, very touching.

Birds, cats, people . . . no, we don't stop there. Animals of assorted kinds. George the goat, for instance.

George was one of twin Alpine goats born at Belle Vue zoo. His mother developed mastitis and so was unable to rear her young. Linda, one of the keepers who worked at Belle Vue, took the female twin, Beauty, and we took George. He was four days old when we got him, about the size of a small terrier, sparkling white, dainty as the mythical unicorn, but . . . Well, he already had horns in the making, all he needed was the forked tail; he was a demon.

We took him home in the car, on Pat's knee. She kept saying, 'Isn't he gorgeous?' and giving him a cuddle. George, saying nowt, looked angelic and bided his time.

When we arrived Pat carried him through the house and put him down in the kitchen. All was still for a moment as everyone weighed everyone else up, then George bounded forward and butted the first cat he could find, then the next, then the next. He made a mistake, though, when he came to Tich. Tich was bigger than George, it was his house and, ever since he'd grown to his full size, his favourite trick was butting people.

The two met head on, and George lost. He obviously didn't believe in wasting his time in unequal combat and immediately turned to the Siamese cats again. But Tich was after him and virtually butted him all round the kitchen – the big black cat and the pretty little goat charging about like two escapees from a Disney cartoon while the Siamese sat on chairs and watched. After that George grew crafty, he left Tich alone and only charged the other cats when he was sure Tich wasn't about.

It was obvious there wasn't going to be any peace if we left him downstairs to sleep. On the other hand, it didn't seem fair to shut him up by himself while he was so young and had been used to company in the night. So when we went to bed we took him up with us and put him in a box in the corner of the bedroom.

It was all right for a couple of weeks, since he was well fed and tired after each long day, but young animals grow at an alarming rate and their vitality increases with their size. George started getting up in the night. And he bounced.

Goats do. They spring around on all fours like a very hard rubber ball with legs: bump – bump-bump – all round the bed in the small hours of the morning. 'He does it all day,' Pat moaned. 'And now at night, too. I can't stand it.'

Neither could I. George and his box were moved to the bathroom at night. If he bounced all round that it was too far away for us to hear.

In the evenings, if he wasn't charging after the cats or being chased by Tich, he'd lie quietly on the floor like a dog, sometimes rubbing his head against my legs. This was all right until his horns started to come through, which they did at a very early age. I learned to get my legs out of the way pretty smartly when he made a sharp upward movement with his head, although too often I wasn't quick enough and for a few weeks had permanently bruised shins.

One evening he wandered up to the gas fire, which had just been lit, and stood basking in its warmth. He liked it; he liked it so much that he made himself comfortable by leaning against the wire guard. A smell of burning goat hair gradually permeated the air and Pat grabbed him and removed him bodily. His lovely white coat had a scorch line along it. 'What on earth is Peter going to say when he sees him?' Pat said. We were taking George back for a visit to the zoo that weekend.

'Oh, well, it's not too much. It'll probably have grown out by then,' I said.

It hadn't. It was fainter but it was a definite scorch mark along the top of his body when Pat carried him into the zoo a few days later. Linda was there with Beauty, George's twin. Pat was about to say something when she stopped and looked at Beauty. Linda was looking at George. 'You've got a gas fire, haven't you?' she said.

'Yes. So have you, I see,' Pat answered.

Beauty had exactly the same scorch mark in exactly the same place.

112

Neither of the two goats could be discouraged from warming themselves till it hurt; every weekend Linda and Pat compared notes. As the goats grew taller the marks descended, fading in layers from the top of their bodies, but it wasn't until some time after they'd been returned to the zoo that their coats grew back to sparkling whiteness.

George was reared on milk, which he sucked from a bottle. It was supposed to be his main diet until he went on solids: pellets, oats, bran and the like, at about five weeks. But he put himself on solids without waiting for us, and he ate anything. Goats do that, too. The tablecloth, the curtains, newspapers, cushions – whatever he got a chance to digest he'd have a go at, and we simply couldn't stop him.

At six weeks old he was bouncing, butting, roasting himself nightly and eating everything with reach. Our shins bruised and our nerves wracked, we wrestled with him one day. I held him in a sort of leg lock while Pat prised what was left of a tea towel from his steadily masticating jaws. 'He's got to go,' she said to me.

'By God, he has. He can look after himself now, anyway,' I agreed.

'Look after himself,' she repeated faintly. 'Look after himself. He'll *destroy* us if we don't get him out of here.'

So George went, and an exhausted and much appreciated peace settled over the house once more.

Eleven

Fred

The cats, having grown up with birds, not only take them for
granted, they play with them and compete for our attention –
more than once I've seen two cats and a bird crammed together
on Pat's lap. And when their mothering instincts come to the
surface, they take care of them.

Fred, the barn owl, came to us as the most beautiful and
helpless little creature I've ever seen. He had been found by
someone in mid-Cheshire and handed in to the RSPCA, who
had brought him to us. He was a fluffy little chick, no more than
two weeks old, perfectly formed but paralysed to such an extent
he was able to move only his head. Pesticides again, of the type
that attack the motor cells in the brain. His mother must have
caught infected vermin and fed them to her young. No doubt
she had died, the other chicks, too, and only Fred was left.

He could eat – that is, if we put food in his beak he could swallow. Food was really the only thing he was interested in. He
didn't bother at all about us, the other birds round him, or the
cats. The cats, however, took a great interest in him, giving him
the occasional wash and nestling against him, keeping him
warm.

There was no treatment we could give him. We asked advice
but there was nothing we could do except feed him – as we
always did with very sick birds – on a high protein diet. Birds
store poisons in their body fats, and if a bird thins down the
poison is released into the system. I try to make the process
work in reverse, building up a good fatty deposit so that the
poison is contained rather than distributed round the body.
This worked with Fred, and very gradually some use returned

to his body. At first he could stretch out his wings, then he could make faint motions with them that slowly evolved into a paddling action, similar to the sort of movement a swimmer performs doing the butterfly stroke.

All the time, Fred was growing, turning from a downy little bundle into an exquisitely plumaged bird, creamy white on his chest, his wings and back the most subtle shadings of grey and brown and russet gold; his face was the beautiful heart shape of the barn owl, white, fringed with gold. A bird can move almost every feather on its body by means of the dermal, or skin muscles – these are what enable them to use their feathers for flight and display and so on. By infinitesimal rearrangements of his facial muscles and feathers Fred was capable of an astonishing range of expressions, almost human in their effect.

Once his strength had built up he began to get about, his legs remained useless, the thigh muscles never developed at all, but he made his wings work for him, their paddling action pulling him along. Then he learned to flutter – never more than an inch clear of the floor; when we watched him at this we hoped that some use was returning to his legs because very often the fluttering movement was deceptive – he seemed to be walking. But he wasn't, his legs had virtually atrophied and we knew our waiting and hoping was futile. He improved to a certain stage but never progressed beyond it. It would have taken a miracle for him to do so, the paralysis had been too severe in the first place; it was a wonder he lived so long and got about the way he did.

At first he spent his nights sleeping in a box, although after a while he usually managed to get out and go and join the cats and snuggle in with them. During the day he pottered about on the floor, towing himself around by his wings. I'm sure he thought he was a cat because they virtually brought him up and as long as he lived, almost three years, they were his companions. Big as they were in contrast to his small body they were always gentle with him and never frightened him. There was one night, though, when he managed to frighten himself pretty thoroughly.

I was out late and Pat had gone up to bed by herself when

suddenly the quiet of the house was shattered by a frantic clattering, a metallic sound unlike anything she'd ever heard before. She rushed downstairs and put the kitchen light on. Absolute silence greeted her. She looked around, wondering what could have caused the noise. Then it came again, briefly, as if directing her attention. She looked down in the corner where a small metal waste basket stood. From the top of it Fred's face peeped out with an expression that said 'Help' as plainly as any words. Instead of settling down to sleep when everyone else did he'd decided on a spell of pottering and somehow – we never knew how and he never did it again – managed to flutter high enough to get inside the waste basket without tipping it over. It was empty, so he had nothing to stand on to launch himself out again. He'd just popped down inside it and had to wait to be rescued.

He enjoyed the company of human beings as well as cats, sitting on Pat's knee, or mine – or, for that matter, wherever he felt like on any visitor who didn't object, and few people could resist him. His beautiful appearance and indefinable air of 'character' made him one of the most enchanting birds we've ever had. When he was put on a stranger's knee he'd sit there and regard them unblinkingly for long, long minutes, narrowing and widening his eyes and pulling faces, as if he was trying to make up his mind to further their acquaintance. He always did, he was a friendly soul.

By a slow series of wing paddlings, with many pauses for thought, he'd make his way up until he came to rest somewhere in the region of the visitor's chest. Hooking his claws into whatever it was – a jersey, a jacket, a dress, he'd nestle close, tucking his head under their chin and settle down to rest there, downy and weightless and warm. Many a friend chatted away the entire evening wearing the little barn owl like a muffler.

Pat and I are not qualified vets, as I point out to everyone who brings a bird to us, every time suggesting they first consult a vet. Time without number the answer comes back, 'Oh, we've been to see Mr X, he sent us to you, you're the specialist.' Well, I'm not, I'm a hobbyist and enthusiast, call it what you like, but one thing I'd never set myself up to be is a specialist.

It's true that I've handled hundreds of different types of birds over the years but I've always been aware that there are gaps in my knowledge, that there is still a great deal for me to learn. However, it is a sad fact that many vets refuse point blank to treat a wild bird and there are several reasons for this.

The domestic vet who has his surgery in town or suburb treats cats, dogs, rabbits – the general run of family pet, and very often simply isn't interested in birds. The demands of his practice don't allow him to put in the time that Pat and I give to nursing injured birds back to health or rearing owl chicks – just to set them free at the end of it. There's the question of cost, too; we're not making a business pay, a vet is.

During the course of a weekend – say from Friday evening to Sunday – we can have as many as eight different types of birds brought to us: foundlings, fledgelings, the lame, the starving, the sick, the wounded – anything. The well-meaning individuals who bring them to us – generally, as I said, after having been told by a vet that nothing can be done – might have travelled miles in their effort to track down someone who can help the injured bird they have found, and thank God there are people who care, who will always care. We never turn anyone away, we can't, we don't know how to say 'Take it somewhere else, there's no room here.' But I can count on the fingers of one hand the number of people who give a thought to the consequences of their action, to the everyday, economical realities: who pays for the treatment? Who pays for the foodstuff? Who pays?

Quite simply, Pat and I do. We know that the bird brought to us can be in our home a day, a month, a year, several years, it becomes our responsibility, dependent on us, that's something we just take as a matter of course. A vet, faced with the same situation, knows this, too. He's running a practice, not a sanctuary; you can't send bills to strangers who dump a box of owlets on your step and disappear into the night.

There are animal welfare societies, any number of them, supported by contributions and staffed by volunteers. A great deal of their work goes into picking up and looking after strays and finding homes for them; a lot of cats and dogs would live wretchedly if it weren't for the efforts of these societies. When it comes to injured animals, though, they have no resources to treat anything but minor complaints and have to consult vets, some of whom will reduce their fees for such cases. The RSPCA do wonderful work as well, although most of their branches are under-staffed and coping with an unwieldy workload, which is why they have to rely on private individuals taking in animals that would otherwise have to be put down.

I've come to know a lot of vets, just a few very well, and they've pointed out to me that their inability to turn themselves into voluntary hospitals has resulted in a lack of experience in treating wild birds. There are good vets and bad vets, it's unrealistic to pretend otherwise. The bad ones unfortunately are not only not interested, they're extraordinarily ignorant, too I know personally of one who refused to treat a buzzard that was taken to his surgery, giving as his reason, 'I can't touch that, it's a tropical bird.' Another wondered why a heron wouldn't eat when he tried to feed it on tinned pilchards in tomato sauce. Others have said quite frankly that wild birds are just not popular enough for any vet to waste his time specialising in, and they admit that their advice to anyone who brings them a kestrel, owl or the like is to have it put down.

Many vets I've come to know within range of us are acting for the best when they send people along to us. It isn't that they don't want to bother, or are thinking of who is going to pay for sometimes prolonged and costly treatment, it is that they weigh their theoretical knowledge against our practical experience and know there are injuries and diseases we have successfully treated in the past. There can also be puzzling aspects to a case which would make considerable demands on the time they have to give to their practices. It's a fair chance that whatever it is, we are quite likely to have come across it before, and know what to do. This is not, as I said earlier, because we are experts, our capabilities are limited, and we're always very much aware of this. But in our own subject our range has become extensive, we've probably had more birds through our hands in twenty-three years than the average vet will see in a lifetime.

When I've had one of these problem cases sent to me, or when there's something I want to attempt but am not sure of, I can turn to one or two vets who are personal friends and ask for advice. They'll readily talk things over and make suggestions; by pooling our knowledge in this way we generally come up with the answer.

There was a time when I had brought to me a Greylag goose that had been shot in the right leg. It was obvious that she'd had the injury some time. The leg itself had simply gone rotten, the ends of the broken bone were sticking out and had worn smooth where they'd rubbed against each other. It was also obvious, when I looked at her, that the injury was too severe and complicated for me to tackle. The animal welfare society that had brought her to me had an agreement with one of our local vets that they could take urgent cases to him out of surgery hours. I knew this was one such case so, although it was after nine in the evening, I drove round and knocked him up.

The resident vet was away on holiday but he had a locum in, a young man from Scotland who, by good luck, had a great interest in birds and no objection to treating one in his time off. After he'd examined the goose he pointed out to me that as the break was so bad, and so high – about at the point of the thigh, he had no choice but to amputate the leg, a job he'd never done before. He was quite willing to start at once and asked me if I'd like to stay and lend a hand. Naturally, I said yes.

It was a tricky operation, and a long one. He removed the leg and built a fatty pad on the end of the limb in the hope that when the wound healed it would be possible to fit an artificial limb. This, unfortunately, proved to be impracticable. However, he worked skilfully and sympathetically into the small hours, I think it was about four in the morning before he'd finished. I was pretty tired myself by then just acting as assistant, so goodness knows how he felt.

I told him how grateful I was and how much I appreciated what he had done. 'How much?' I asked, getting my coat on.

'Well . . .' he answered, 'it was a really interesting job, I've never done one quite like that, as I said. Just pay me for the drugs.'

That, as I recall, amounted to four or five pounds, beyond that he would take nothing for all the time he had spent. After the operation it was essential the goose was kept out of water for at least three weeks, and she also needed somewhere to convalesce and learn to get about safely on one leg. For her well-being she needed space, quiet and a soft, dry surface. Where?

The livingroom next door, backing on to our kitchen and now incorporated into the rest of the house by means of the entrance we'd made through the wall – that was where, obviously. Pat and I cleaned it out. We carried all the furniture into other rooms, took up the carpet and bought a load of straw to spread from wall to wall. It was an ideal hospital ward but – after a time – we thought perhaps a little lonely for the Greylag; some gentle company of one of her own kind would do her good, and we had just the answer in Baby, a Canada goose.

I'd been away in Ireland when Pat took the Canada goose in. It had been found in Urmston, a few miles away, wandering about the street and going in and out of shops. By the time I got back home it had established itself in the aviary, a really handsome young bird, greyish brown, with a dapper black head and sparkling white chin patch.

Canada geese are quite common, being residents of the British Isles, sociable birds living in large flocks. I would say, though, that they are uncommon as singletons in shopping centres, and this one – Baby we called him – turned out to be far from the usual run of goose in another respect as well.

He was a charming creature, gentle and friendly. There didn't seem to be anything at all wrong with him but, just to be on the safe side – and until we found a home for him – we decided to keep him in the aviary for a while. There was no pond there though, and he needed one, so I dug a hole and lined it and filled it with water. He had food, space, somewhere to swim and no enemies and we took it for granted he would be perfectly all right. Then, after he had been with us a couple of days we went to the aviary one morning and looked in – and there was no Canada goose. There are a few odd shelters and corners where the smaller birds might conceal themselves but nowhere of a size adequate enough to conceal a Canada goose.

'Where's Baby?' Pat asked, bewildered.

'He's got to be here *somewhere*,' I said, busy unlocking the door. I was as puzzled as she was.

The only place we could think of looking in was the pond – and there, just above the surface of the water – was the goose's beak. We got him out, fortunately in good time, he could only just have gone under . . . But why? A goose that sank? It seemed absurd. We took him indoors and dried him off, the completely sodden state of his feathers and the fact that neither of us had actually seen him on the pond before gave us the clue to the trouble.

By some genetic defect, the goose had no oil gland. This is a small orifice sited just above the tail; a bird, when it preens itself, reaches back and with its beak presses the gland, releasing oil that adheres to the beak and is then transfered to the feathers by the preening action. Spreading this oil regularly over itself a bird insulates its plumage and – most important in waterfowl – waterproofs itself as well. Baby thought he had this gland, he preened himself meticulously because that was what nature had programmed him to do, but he was going through the motions, that was all; in reality he was completely unprotected – and not only because he lacked the waterproofing that would keep out the wet as he paddled about. A bird's plumage is made up of thousands of feathers of varying types, so many, in fact, their total weight exceeds that of the bird's body. In consequence, a thorough soaking of such a mass, accumulating the weight the goose had to carry while afloat, would hamper him more and more and drag him down – virtually the same situation as a human being tipped overboard fully clothed.

I filled in the pond straightaway, the best favour anyone can do for a goose that can't swim. After that the only time he got wet was when it rained, and then if there was a real downpour he got so waterlogged he couldn't support his own weight and fell over and we had to bring him in and dry him by the fire.

He was, as I said, the ideal companion for the convalescing Greylag and the two happily shared the straw-covered livingroom for a month. By then the Greylag's leg was completely healed and she'd adapted herself to getting about on it, so we put both geese in the aviary together.

They were companions for years, and in fact Baby is still with us, but we noticed after a few years that the Greylag was weakening. She was pretty elderly when she came to us so it was apparent that old age was overtaking her. Anyone who knows birds can sense their inner vitality, how it moderates and changes with their health and age; it's nothing to do with behaviour or appearance, it is something indefinable that communicates itself to those of us who care for them. It was autumn, and with winter coming on we worried about the Greylag getting through it. We talked about bringing her indoors when the weather showed signs of getting colder; we could keep her in the bathroom during the worst of the winter – after all, what is a bathroom for if not to provide shelter for an old friend?

We discussed this for a couple of days then one evening Pat said, 'Tomorrow, I think. She looks to be getting a bit weak to me. I'll get the bathroom ready tomorrow and you bring her in.'

I agreed. But it was one of those occasions when nature, or fate, or time, takes over from human arrangements. The Greylag had run her alloted span, when I went into the aviary the next morning it was to find her dead in her little straw-filled corner.

Twelve

'I like you, crow.'

One day I received a phone call asking for help from a man who lived some ten miles away. He had been in touch with the RSPCA who had put him on to me. The problem, he explained, was that his old uncle was going into hospital, leaving at home his two companions, a cat and a crow. Someone had offered a home for the cat, but the crow. . . . Well, crows were pretty hard to place as lodgers, especially old ones, accustomed to the company of a single human being for over twenty years and not exactly keen on strangers.

'Bring it along,' I said. 'We'll look after it for the old gentleman.'

So Charles arrived; he had the scruffy look of the ancient he was, an irascible air and terrible feet. As I understood it, he had been found as a fledgeling, having fallen from his nest or been deliberately rejected; he had never flown and walked or hopped everywhere. His claws had become so overgrown they had curled right round.

I attended to the claws right away, clipping and trimming while Pat held the crow. He squirmed, screeched and – furious at the indignity of his position – made the only positive protest he could by pecking at Pat's hands. When we had finished we put him down on the floor. After glaring about at the cats he hobbled up to one that had unwisely turned away and gave it a sharp prod in the bottom with his two inch beak. It yelped with indignation and dived for cover. The others withdrew, they could take a hint.

Coming as he did from a bachelor establishment and fretting

for his absent master, Charles looked to me for the sympathetic assurance he so badly needed and right from the start overwhelmed me with affection. At night he slept in the extension on top of an old sideboard. It was on the morning after the first night he had spent with us that I went downstairs and was startled by a gruff cry of 'How are you?' I stood still, wondering if someone in the street outside was calling a greeting to a friend. Then the cry came again, 'How are you?' I looked towards the extension. Peering in through the window was Charles.

So that was it. We had been told the crow talked – in imitation of his old master – though his store of words was limited. I gave him a wave, called a greeting suitably restrained to ten past five in the morning and prepared to pass on to the scullery to kettle, teapot, shave, and all the routine of the beginning of the day. But Charles didn't know anything about routine. He had seen me and, croaking his increasingly raucous 'How are you?' and jumping up and down with excitement, he was determined that I should go in and see *him*.

I gave in. The crow had been uprooted from a home he had known for twenty years, he was bound to be unsettled . . . and, anyway, no bird that demanded my notice demanded it in vain. I went through to the extension. It would have been churlish to cut short the welcome so generously given by the gruff, friendly bird – one minute became two, then three, then four – it was five minutes before Charles was satisfied with his share of attention and, quietening down, he let me go, peering after me with his bright old eyes.

The first morning established the pattern for those that followed; I had to set my alarm five minutes earlier to give myself extra time to organise my chores and talk to Charles. And at the other end of the day Charles was no less demonstrative. If he could be near me he was content, and in the evenings, perching on the back of my armchair and thrusting his beak practically in my ear, he carried on a long, confidential conversation – muted, meaningless sounds we called 'chunner'.

Pat's natural rapport with birds didn't work where Charles was concerned. He wasn't accustomed to women, and too crotchety to change his ways in a hurry, but change them he would, she was determined about that. During the day he kept to himself, hunched up and brooding; as Pat went about her work in the house she would from time to time hear his voice, hoarse and penetrating, pitched to an old man's tone – 'I like you, crow.'

'*I* like you, crow,' she would call back. But Charles wasn't having any of this fraternising business. When she was in the room he glared and occasionally screeched, and when she got within range he pecked her feet.

If he was on a higher level – on the bookcase or the sideboard – he pecked anywhere else he could reach, too: her hands, her arms, her neck – the angry beak darted forward, snatching a piece of flesh and twisting it. Covered in blood blisters out refusing to give up, Pat went on making friendly overtures, standing in front of him – ready to dodge – and repeating, 'I like you, crow.' If he occasionally responded with the other item of his extremely restricted repertoire: 'I *don't* like you, crow,' she would answer, 'Well I do, you daft bird, so you might as well get used to the idea.'

Eventually, he did, he had no choice – Pat wasn't moving cut for any crow. She fed him and talked to him, and because she was about the house all day he gradually grew to tolerate her company, then to accept it, then to enjoy it.

One evening I poured myself a pint of beer and sat down to enjoy it. After a couple of sips I put the mug on the floor beside my chair and at once, as if at a signal, Charles gave an impassioned screech and hurtled across the kitchen, wings out, making straight for the mug. It was at that moment I remembered that the man who had brought the crow mentioned he 'liked a drop of ale'. Demonstrating this without any possibility of error, Charles skidded to a halt, dipped his head into the mug and with all the relish of one long deprived of necessary sustenance, started slurping.

'Hold on,' I said. But Charles was a stranger to the meaning of moderation and had to be forcibly separated from the mug. How much he is capable of drinking remains forever a matter of speculation. Possibly he would carry on till he fell over, but he has never been given the opportunity. It would be cruelly unfair to allow him to drink to the point of inebriation. The idea of a drunk crow might be amusing but the reality would be distressing in the extreme. So Charles is occasionally allowed his 'drop of ale' – just that, and no more.

For his diet, he ate anything put before him, with a distinct preference for baked beans. But it very quickly became apparent that the food he liked best was the food he stole: the cats' food, the kestrels' – anything he could lay his beak to, and what he couldn't eat, he hoarded.

I discovered this one day when I trod on the carpet and it squelched. I had no idea what could be under it. In a house like ours, with livestock all over the place, I dared not pretend I hadn't noticed anything and go away. It sounded unpleasant, but I had to look and when I got down on my hands and knees I discovered that the corner of the carpet had been painstakingly picked away until it could be lifted. Underneath it was a squashed grape. I didn't have much doubt about the identity of the culprit, as the crow family are notorious for their habit of stealing and hoarding.

I told Pat and she said, 'Ho. I'll keep an eye on that gentleman,' but it was some time before she caught Charles returning to his hiding place in search of the grape – and reacting very angrily to the disappearance of his loot. In a fit of pique – or possibly an idle moment when he could think of nothing else to do – he ripped a strip of wallpaper from the wall and hid that under the carpet. After that Pat had to expend considerable energy diving at him to discourage him in the act before he stripped all the wallpaper at crow level round the kitchen.

Deprived of one hiding place, dissuaded, or missing the treasures he had so carefully stowed away, Charles occasionally resorted to desperate measures. Keeping out of sight (with what might have been deliberate cunning) of Pat's watchful eye, he spent some time in a recess of the chimney breast, pulling the vinyl paper away above the skirting board and digging in a hole in the exposed plaster. This cranny was so inconspicuous (the vinyl paper, being stiff and undamaged, simply fell back into place when he stopped poking about behind it) that he might have made use of it indefinitely – if he hadn't chosen to tuck a piece of meat in it. The warmth of the room and the process of decomposition combined to produce a smell that set Pat frantically hunting. Her nose led her to the spot.

A disgruntled Charles watched his snack being disposed of and his hiding place repaired. As she scolded him Pat wondered where on earth he would choose next. He returned to base – so to speak – the carpet, and as long as he stuck to that we all knew where we were. But he must have grown so thoroughly fed up at being constantly foiled that he changed tactics.

One evening Pat saw him busily occupied with a cardigan she had thrown over a chair. 'What's he doing?' she asked me.

'Playing, I suppose,' I answered. Because Charles had his games, purposeless, ferreting antics or – something with more excitement to it – pottering up to a sleeping cat and yanking its tail with his sharp beak. This time I was wrong, Charles wasn't playing, as Pat discovered when she went to put on the cardigan. He had hidden a piece of meat up the sleeve.

Having his claws attended to improved the state of his feet. They straightened out gradually and his walk became very much better. But however his mobility and his circumstances changed, there was one thing about Charles that remained constant – his bedtime.

Until we understood this we wondered why – at ten o'clock – Charles lost interest in everyone and everything, voluntarily relinquished his perch on my chair and pottered about on the floor with a grumpiness that increased as the minutes went by. 'Chunnering' to himself, he walked over to the back door and waited for a while before beginning to patrol backwards and forwards. When this restless, grumbling behaviour evoked no response he ran out of patience entirely, stalked back to the middle of the room and began pecking indiscriminately at feet and cats. Shoo'd off and scolded he still returned, until Pat said, 'Put him to bed, for heaven's sake.'

I picked him up, carried him into the extension and plonked him on the sideboard. Charles knew that that was where he slept, he knew ten o'clock was his bedtime, and without any more fuss at all he settled down for the night.

At ten o'clock the next evening – and the next – he made such a nuisance of himself that he had to be put in the extension. The regularity of this behaviour made me recognise the simple truth: Charles wasn't being awkward for the sake of it, he was being awkward deliberately, to achieve a specific result. He might be prepared to make his home in a strange household, but he was going to give everyone hell if they didn't put him to bed at a respectable hour.

The police call regularly on business of some sort – so regularly there always seems to be at least one permanently parked on the sofa behind a mug of coffee. Shortly after we got Charles a couple of the local bobbies brought their new Inspector round to say hallo. It was a quiet evening for a change, with not too many interruptions from the door or the phone, so the five of us could sit and chat. In fact, we were so busy talking that Pat and I were a bit slow on the uptake when Charles started bothering about all over the place – thinking of his bedtime, of course, which we weren't. Finally, completely fed-up, Charles pattered over to a pair of ankles and started pecking them, *really* pecking, he meant it. An anguished cry broke from the lips of the new Inspector – 'What – what the – what's it *doing?*'

Pat dived for Charles and grabbed him. 'I'm sorry. It's his bedtime, you see, and we forgot . . .'

One of the constables, assisting her, hissed, 'Couldn't the damn thing have gone for one of us? Why did it have to choose the Inspector?'

'Well, he was *nearest*,' Pat said, bearing the crow away to his sideboard. After all, he was only a bird, how could he be expected to appreciate differences in rank?

After six weeks Charles' old master was discharged from hospital and came round to see us. He was by no means well enough to take on the care of the bird but he wanted to reassure himself that his old companion was not fretting too much. He was astonished to find how Charles had settled in and become attached to us; he was pleased, too, I think, and very relieved. He asked if it would be all right if he left him with us 'a little longer', not specifying an exact period.

Crows are funny creatures. In proof of his eccentric disposition, Charles showed no distress at the visit of the master he'd known for twenty years. He settled back with us, fit, happy and irascible . . . we might have been once a temporary refuge but now we were his home.

At one time falconry was a sport confined to royalty and the nobility. Four or five hundred years ago, I understand, any member of the lower orders who took a wild falcon was liable to the most severe punishment, the death penalty.

Nowadays, of course, things are very different. But it wasn't until the nineteenth century that people became aware of the need to protect birds from indiscriminate slaughter for sport and ornamentation. All those glass cases of stuffed birds beloved of the Victorians, the fantastically feathered hats of Edwardian gentlewomen – these were an accepted part of a social scene that also saw the gradual awakening of public conscience.

In latter years great emphasis has been put on the need to conserve our diminishing wildlife and yet many people who most sincerely and wholeheartedly support this aim aren't aware that there are legal requirements to go with it. For instance, as I've mentioned before, any individual who takes a perfectly healthy wild bird from its natural surroundings and keeps it as a pet is acting in contravention of the law and is liable to punishment by fine or – in cases of exceptionally rare species – fine and imprisonment.

The Protection of Birds Act 1954 is lengthy and complicated, necessarily so because its range has to be extensive and it makes provision for the protection of birds in various ways. To put things at their very simplest: it is an offence not only to take a fledgeling from its nest, but also to trap any bird, to kill or injure it. Nests which are in use are protected, so, of course, are eggs. You are permitted to take charge of a bird that has been found injured purely for the purpose of tending it and releasing it when it is no longer disabled. Even so, under this Act, no one may keep a bird in a cage that is too small to permit freedom of movement.

Obviously, there are exceptions to any law and in recognition of these exceptions special licences are issued or certain people or bodies are acknowledged to have authority in specific areas – the Nature Conservancy Council, the Ministry of Agriculture, the RSPCA, the RSPB, falconers, sanctuaries, collectors and so on. There are, for instance, cases where someone who has a collection of wild fowl discovers that a nest has been abandoned at breeding time. It is perfectly legitimate, therefore, for him – as an authorised person – to take the eggs from that nest, hatch them out, rear the chicks and, when they are capable of fending for themselves, return them to the pond or wood or whatever their natural surroundings happen to be.

Our legal system may be cumbersome but it is there to be invoked for the protection of our increasingly threatened wildlife. Of course there are loopholes in the Protection of Birds Act, and of course certain unscrupulous people, for their own ends, will ignore it, that is a sad fact of human nature we have to live with. A lot of birds change hands illegally and a young hawk, ready for training, can cost a great deal of money. Unfortunately, in my experience, the kind of people who are prepared to go to any lengths to obtain a bird aren't willing to give the time and effort it takes to learn to care for it properly; in consequence the bird suffers in captivity and either dies or escapes into the wild in a condition that makes it unfit to survive.

One such case, by no means uncommon, was of a young kestrel that some children saw in a tree in their school yard. It was hanging upside down from a branch and the fluttering of the poor creature's wings as it dangled there caught the children's attention. The RSPCA were called, they went along with the Fire Brigade, took the bird down and brought it to us. How did it come to be trapped there, to die of terror or starvation or as the helpless prey of a cat?

Well, it had jesses on, so someone had had it as a falconer's bird. When a hawk is on the screen perch or block its jesses are held together by a small gadget, shaped like a figure eight,

132

called a swivel, to which the leash is also attached. When the bird is in training, say on the creance, the swivel is removed because, in effect, it acts as a hobble. If there's a mishap and the leash or creance break, the bird is away; this is why immense care must be taken by any falconer or would-be falconer to see that no bird is lost with a swivel. With its legs fastened together its chances of survival are minimal, it has lost a degree of mobility, particularly if short jesses are being used but, much worse, sooner or later it is bound to hook itself on to a branch – just as this kestrel in the school yard had done.

In its panic-stricken efforts to get free it had broken one of its legs and, completely exhausted, toppled off the branch and hung from it – a terrifying experience and one that would have ended in death if the children had not seen it in time.

Thirteen

The nursery stairs

There seemed to be a time when we felt we couldn't move for convalescing kestrels. Wondering what on earth to do with them all Pat had the idea of taking them through to the other part of the house and putting them on the stairs, one to each stair, where it was much quieter than being next to the kitchen and there was plenty of room for them to get about if they wanted to. Feeding time in the evening – or butty time as we usually call it – was quite a performance for Pat. She'd get a big bowl of food ready in the extension, carry it through the house to the top of the stairs and start from there, working her way down one step at a time until all the invalids had had their ration.

Before they reached the stage where they could be put there they'd had to be kept around the kitchen in boxes, or on the floor, until they were mobile enough not to hurt themselves as they explored the stairs.

There was Kelly, who came from Derbyshire. An official of the RSPB knew where there was a nest of four kestrel chicks and had been keeping an eye on them. One day when he went to check up the nest was empty. By a combination of good luck and dogged sleuthing he was able to trace where the chicks had gone, recover them and put them back in the nest. The next day when he went to look, they'd disappeared again. This time he had no luck in tracing their whereabouts but after a short time had passed a friend told him that he knew of someone who was in possession of a young kestrel. There was no way of knowing if it was one of this particular four, however, the fact was that it had been taken illegally and was being kept in conditions likely to cause it suffering. The RSPB official reclaimed it and passed it on to us.

Kelly was not old enough to fly. She couldn't walk, either. She'd been fed only on scraps and as a result of this inadequate diet had developed rickets. There was no use in her legs at all when she came to us, she couldn't even stand, she could only sit on a cushion and rock – pathetically like one of those toys that sway backwards and forwards but don't fall over. She lived in the kitchen on the floor and as her strength returned she began to use her wings to get herself about, in a sort of rowing action. Bit by bit the use returned to her legs. At first she could stand, then she could walk, but the impoverished diet had taken its toll. Her legs were bowed, like those of a child with rickets, and her feet had turned inwards, crossing over each other. Halfway through her convalescence she went to live on the stairs and made way for another invalid, Kizzy.

A young fellow turned up at Belle Vue one day with a very scruffy looking kestrel. He didn't know what to do with it, its feathers kept breaking off. He'd found this kestrel as a chick and, quite ignorant of the fact that he was committing an offence, had kept her as a pet. She'd been living in his garden shed for over a year; when he decided he would turn her loose he realised that with the appalling state of her feathers and her flight no more than a mere flutter she would have very little chance of survival.

It hadn't occurred to him there was a connection between a bird's diet and its ability to grow the strong plumage necessary for its flight and body insulation. By feeding Kizzy on nothing but scraps he'd rendered her virtually flightless. He couldn't recognise hunger traces or understand why her feathers were so brittle they broke off at a touch. He had no idea, either, that in taking and keeping her he'd been on the wrong side of the law.

We took her home and put her on the stairs for a while. She had plenty of space there but we wanted to keep her among the other invalids so that we could be sure she got her food. If we'd put her in the aviary the stronger birds would have stolen it from her. She was very run down and dejected to begin with but after a while she perked up. Her high protein diet was doing her

136

good generally but when it came to her first moult we could see that it hadn't done much for her feathers. The new ones still showed hunger traces, they kept snapping off – not as badly as before but we went on finding bits of them all over the place. We continued to feed her as well as we could and with each moult there was an improvement. After a while she was able to go outdoors to the aviary in conditions closer to her natural ones; soon, we hope, she'll be able to go free.

Dizzy was the next kestrel.

Some children playing in a field in Stalybridge saw a bird walking about in the grass, obviously unable to fly. They went home and told their parents who came out to look and, finding the bird still there, picked it up and took it to a vet. In the vet's opinion there was nothing much wrong with the kestrel apart from a sprained wing, all it needed was a couple of weeks rest and it would be flying again.

The family took her home and looked after her for two weeks . . . then three, at the end of which she still showed no sign of flying. It was becoming difficult for them to keep the bird and they were worried about her. Somehow they found out about us and telephoned me and told me the story. They asked if I could take it off their hands and look after it until it was better; I said yes and the following evening drove over to Stalybridge to collect it.

As soon as I saw Dizzy I knew she would never fly again. Her wing wasn't sprained, it had been broken and set itself, but in such a way that the joint between the forearm and upper arm was immovable, the wing had folded back on itself and it was impossible to open it out.

I took her back with me and introduced her to the other residents. She was a young bird, in her first year's plumage, and after a spell on the stairs soon adapted and began to explore the rest of the house, walking and hopping about wherever her fancy took her, squabbling with the other kestrels, well able to defend her food against thieves.

To give her a change of scenery sometimes we'd put her on top of the bookcase where she'd sit, happily viewing everyone from this unaccustomed elevation, or patrol up and down. Occasionally, she'd attempt to fly, launching herself off the end of

137

the bookcase, but the only mobility she had in her broken wing amounted to the three inch stump of her upper arm; the lower arm carrying her flight feathers remained locked. Using her good wing to break her fall she'd descend in a corkscrew action, rather rapidly, and making something of a bump on landing, but she learned to manage like that and never hurt herself.

The next temporary occupant of the nursery stairs was another young kestrel, Yum-yum. Some people had found him with a shot wing and taken him to a vet. Like the people with Dizzy they did what they could but weren't able to keep the bird and, looking around for someone to take care of it, chanced to hear about us. Pat and I went up to collect Yum-yum. He'd been living indoors and was sitting on a bowl of fruit on the sideboard, looking very much the boss – but that was Yum-yum, a cheeky, bright little bird that had won the hearts of the family. Anxious to do the best for him they told us that the vet had set his wing and it would soon be healed. They also gave us the antibiotic powder that had been prescribed, on the vet's advice, to be sprinkled in the bird's drinking water . . .

As I said before, there are good vets and bad vets, and when I heard that this method of administering powder had been recommended I had a pretty fair indication whereabouts on the scale this particular vet came. Birds of prey *never* drink water – they take all the moisture they need from the meat they eat. In all the years I've kept kestrels, buzzards and owls, the only one I've seen dip a beak in water is Perdita, and that's just before she has her bath. Even so, she's not drinking. As far as I can tell she's just testing the temperature, the way a human being will first check to see if the water's not too hot by dipping a hand in.

So the antibiotic prescribed for Yum-yum had been of no benefit at all. Once we got him home we put the powder on his meat and he took it that way. He was a great eater, his own food and everyone else's. He might not be able to fly but he could run like the blazes. We only had to offer one of the cats something and he'd tear in, grab it and be off at breakneck speed.

We'd only had him a day, though, when we noticed that wherever he went a peculiar and unpleasant smell went with him. I decided to check up on his wing. I didn't much like the look of the way it had been done up, it appeared to be stuck with sellotape. I found it hard to believe a vet would use such a thing, although it was difficult to tell how it had been put on as the whole area of the wound was very messy.

Pat held Yum-yum while I removed the 'dressing'. It was sellotape, and as I cut it away the smell became almost overpowering. I've never seen such a mess. The two raw ends of the upper and forearm bones had been brought together, the broken connecting joint laid on top – quite separate – and this whole portion of the shot wing stuck with sellotape. As a result, no air could get to the wound, it had literally gone rotten, and by rotten I mean maggotty. I won't dwell on it, it was disgusting. Once the wound was open to the air we could attend to it regularly and very soon it was completely clean and healthy. But the wing had by then set, there was no flexibility in it at all; like Dizzy, Yum-yum was a one-winged bird. But he was strong and young and very fit, a tyrant and unrepentant thief, making up in ground speed what he lacked in air power; in all the time we've had him he's kept up that remarkable sprint to get himself out of trouble.

When we began to think the world was full of kestrels and nothing else, someone brought us a mistle thrush with a broken wing. I set the wing in a splint and put Mizzy, as we called her, in the cage under the stairs with the mynah bird. This pretty, delicate thrush had to go there for her own safety; the cats wouldn't harm her but one or two of the bolder kestrels would probably start eyeing her as a tasty morsel and smacking their lips. We thought, also, that she would have an instinctive fear of them and be intimidated if she found herself loose in a room with them fluttering about her.

When her wing had set we found ourselves disappointed in our hope of releasing her. The break had been a bad one, the mended wing was permanently dropped. This meant she could flutter for short distances but had no staying power, and out in the wild she would have no chance at all. So she had to stay. As an experiment we let her loose in the kitchen and kept an eye on her – and on the kestrels.

Thrushes are supposed to be shy creatures . . . Not Mizzy. She was very self-possessed and inquisitive, eager to find her way about, and a vigorous scold if anyone tried to interfere with her. We watched her exploring her new surroundings. She showed a preference for the top of the bookcase so Pat put a tray of food up there for her. One of the kestrels at once took an interest – either in the food or in Mizzy, which to him could be the same thing. We stood by, ready to do a rescue act. It wasn't necessary. Mizzy wasn't having any old kestrel on her bookcase. She rushed at him, chattering furiously, and he took off. Two more fluttered down. Mizzy put her wings out and went straight for them, shrill with outrage, an unswerving charge that startled them into retreat.

'She's supposed to be afraid of them,' Pat said thoughtfully.

'Well, she isn't. And if we don't tell her, she won't know,' I said.

And that's the way it was; with one exception Mizzy never tolerated anyone or anything on her bookcase. When Pat went to change her food tray at night Mizzy would either peck at her hands or fly across the room to the curtain pelmet and sit there chattering with annoyance until Pat had finished. The kestrels soon gave up trying to trespass. There wasn't one brave enough to tackle the scolding, scampering thrush, she simply wouldn't have anyone on her territory – until we put Dizzy up there.

Poor Dizzy, with her one good wing and the stump that was all she had left of the other. She couldn't fly away from Mizzy but, oddly enough, the thrush never went for her. I don't like to claim it was some primitive recognition at work – I wouldn't say sympathy, but at least tolerance. It was strange that Mizzy could accept a bird more disabled than herself and never once objected to Dizzy sharing her territory.

When Kelly had got over the convalescing stage she had a short spell of living in the kitchen. It was a bit crowded there, what with one thing and another, so, as she was strong enough to look after herself, we put her in the aviary. She hated that. Hunched-up and sulking she stood in a corner on her funny bowed legs, refusing to eat. We left her for a little while, thinking that the change of surroundings had upset her and she would gradually acclimatise herself, but after three days had gone by and she showed no change Pat couldn't stand it any more.

She brought Kelly back in the house and let her have the run of the kitchen. Very soon, however, Kelly went missing. Pat looked for her and found her on the nursery stairs, empty now of invalids.

She didn't attempt to move her. Kelly was out of the way and if she preferred her own company that was up to her. The odd bird or cat would wander there sometimes and occasionally Kelly made a brief visit to the kitchen. On one of these visits she must have discovered the other stairs – the one that go up from the scullery to our bedroom – and we noticed that she began to divide her time between both staircases. Pat noticed particularly, because if she went up or down without her slippers Kelly darted out and pecked her bare feet. Feet shod or covered in whatever fashion Kelly didn't object to, it was bare feet that made her angry.

After a while she moved her quarters permanently from the nursery stairs to the kitchen stairs. We've never had a bird deliberately anti-social, she just doesn't like company – or, at least, if she ever wants any she's extremely selective about it. When we have visitors, or things are going on, she keeps to herself on the stairs. But sometimes, when the house is quiet and Pat is pottering about in the scullery, cleaning or getting a meal ready, there'll be a pattering and fluttering, a disturbance of the curtain across the doorway, then Kelly edges shyly in to spend a little time in Pat's undemanding and sympathetic company.

Fourteen

A hot water bottle and a blanket

We are regular visitors to some friends who own a pig farm at Saddleworth; pigs we know nothing about, as I'd be the first to admit. But one day when we were there we heard of a piglet that had been lost to a litter, and how it came about.

Very small piglets have one thought – food, and they will fight with all their puny strength for the nearest teat of the sow. It can happen that in the general shoving, scrambling and indiscriminate suckling, one teat is not used and this very quickly dries up. When the piglets finally organise themselves according to the mysterious dictates of nature and settle down to their own source of food, one piglet is left with an unproductive teat and simply dies from lack of nourishment.

When we were told about this my sympathy was aroused at once and I incautiously said, 'If you get another one like that we'd like to try and raise it for you.' I knew that the piglet would not be diseased or deformed in any way, simply in need of individual and constant attention – round the clock feeding – and that was something a busy farmer doesn't have the time to provide. When I offered 'we'd like to try and raise it –' Pat repeated the *we* with somewhat sarcastic emphasis; as she was the one at home all day she knew who would be doing the bottle feeding.

But when the chance came, for all her protestations of 'Don't you think I've quite enough to do as it is?' – it was Pat who picked up the wicker cat basket and said, 'We can bring him home in this. Come on, let's go and get him.'

The piglet was a three day old skeleton, five inches high, hungry, fed-up and liberally marked with the scars his fight for life had already cost him. Pat carried him to the car in the cat

143

basket but once there, opening the lid to look at him, she had second thoughts.

'What are you doing?' I asked, as I started the car.

'He's so *tiny* – and so lonely in that big basket . . . He's not travelling all the way home rattling about in it.'

'Well, where . . . ?'

'Where? Where else?' Pat said, and the piglet was out of the basket and under her coat. He settled down there, too dispirited to react to this extraordinary turn of events; but at least he was warm, and burrowing down to make himself comfortable he fell asleep.

On the drive we discussed what we might call him. All kinds of creatures had found a temporary home with us – but never a pig, and in recognition of this unique status he must have a name. 'Poor roly-poly pig,' Pat said – and that was it: Roly.

As soon as we arrived home Pat made up a mixture of sterilised milk, water and glucose and set about feeding him. In theory it was simple, the essentials were there: a feeding bottle with a teat and a ravenous piglet. Getting them together in an effective combination proved to be another matter.

Roly had a snout, and a lower jaw set back from it; this meant that when Pat put the bottle into the front of his mouth it didn't reach far enough for him to suck. She tried it sideways, misjudging its length: the end stuck out of the other side of Roly's mouth and as he grabbed and squeezed the milk went all over Pat's lap. Eventually she settled for a precariously oblique position and as long as she could keep it there Roly sucked with all the fury of his starved little frame. Fine judgement, however, was ill-matched to a squirming piglet and before Roly had had his fill Pat had a fair amount of milk splattered all over her.

But they managed and, replete, his face washed, Roly was set down on the floor to have a look around and make the acquaintance of the cats. He took no notice of them. Full for the first time in his three day old life he was content to do nothing at all; and as Pat said – he was so very young he didn't know the way of the world, cats were just something happened, possibly he took them for furry piglets.

I got his bed ready, filling the cat basket with straw. Then I wound up an old alarm clock, fastened it in a plastic bag to keep dry and put that in the basket. Roly was accustomed to company and slept close to his mother, the steady tick of the alarm clock simulated her heartbeat; alone for the first time in his young life he needed this assurance to get him through the hours of darkness.

By the time other preparations for the night had been made Roly was hungry again, squeaking for more food. Pat went once more through the messy and comic performance and at last tucked the full, sleepy piglet into his basket.

Anxious as I was to check up on the new arrival the first thing I had to do on getting up was spend the obligatory five minutes with Charles, who would give me no peace and rouse the entire household if I dared to try and sneak another job in first. As soon as I could I went to the cat basket to look at Roly. When I touched the piglet I found it stone cold and lifeless, and when I picked it up its body hung limp in my hand. I felt for the heartbeat but could discern nothing at all. The little creature had apparently died in the night.

Pat, too impatient to wait for her progress report and cup of tea, had come downstairs shortly after me, to find me standing in the kitchen with the piglet in my hand. 'I'm afraid he hasn't made it, Trish. I'll take him outside.'

At once she answered, 'He can't be dead. I'm not having him die on us so soon.' Some primitive instinct operates in Pat, it is quite beyond her explanation and has nothing to do with rational thought, optimism, or reluctance to face realities, it is just that on some occasions she *knows* when a creature is going to live. This was one such occasion – and she was right.

As we handled the tiny scrap we detected a faint but unmistakable movement, the merest flicker of response that at once was enough to set us into action. Pat wrapped him in a piece of old blanket and quickly mixed some food, I put on the kettle for a hot water bottle and this ensured his survival.

Roly's priority was food. When he was full he was quiet,

when he was hungry he set up a plaintively persistent squeaking. Pat decided from the beginning that there would be no rigid timetable, she would feed Roly when he squeaked – and for the first few days he did that every half hour. It was with considerable relief that she noticed his demands imperceptibly began to be spaced at longer intervals until he settled for a period of two to three hours.

As soon as he was fit enough to stand the shock – and the indignity – he was given a bath. Furiously put out, he squealed, wriggled and flailed his sharp little trotters; but if he was reliant for his well-being on the benefits of civilised living, he had to make one concession in return: he had to be clean. And clean he eventually was, but I must admit that when it comes to comparisons in the matter of washing, I prefer a guinea pig to a piglet any day. At least you can get hold of fur and hang on to it for a while, but it was impossible to get a handful of Roly, his skin fitted him too tightly.

Roly very soon became attached to Pat, recognising her as a source of food and company. During the day he followed her about, trotting busily after her through the house. He never managed the stairs and wasn't encouraged to try; when she went up to do the bedroom he stood at the bottom of the stairs, protesting at her desertion by a series of increasingly infuriated squeals.

He grew rapidly and was soon too big for the cat basket. Straw wasn't in plentiful supply so we filled a large cardboard box with paper and cut a piece from the side so he had a little doorway to go in and out whenever he wanted. If he wasn't following Pat about, he climbed into his box, scrunched the one or two apples put in for him – of which he was immensely fond – occupied himself shredding every inch of paper, then burrowed down to sleep. When he was a few weeks old we put the box in the extension, although he had the run of the house during the day it was there he spent his nights, happily cluttered with shredded paper, blanket, hot water bottle and, very often, one of the Siamese cats curled up with him.

146

His food was there, too. He progressed from milk to pig pellets – a wet mush he very much enjoyed – and as he shared night quarters with Charles this food inevitably came under the glare of the crow's acquisitive eye. But Charles was disappointed. The pellets, mixed with milk, were too sloppy to be transported and hidden and, to a crow, not very appetising. Roly's apples were a different matter; strangely shaped lumps appearing under the carpet warned us that Charles was up to his usual tricks and Pat was constantly retrieving pieces of apple and returning them to their owner.

In his turn, Roly chanced on the pleasures of pilfering. We had our meals off a low table in the kitchen. When he was very young Roly was far too small to understand, or even see what he was missing; but his size increased rapidly and one day he discovered he was at snout level with the table, a mouthwatering array of delights spread before him. He was helping himself thoughtfully to some bread and butter when Pat caught him. 'Out –' and out he went, to his box in the extension. After that we knew we would never be able to eat in any kind of comfort and at mealtimes Roly had to be banished.

When he was six weeks old it was time for him to return to the farm. We put him in a box, with paper and apples, and carried the box to the car. The journey was made to the noise of scrunched apples, the busy shredding of paper, then the heaving and rustling of Roly burrowing down for a nap.

When we arrived we lifted him out and put him down on the ground. He followed Pat – as always – as we said hello to our friends and then made our way to the sty where Roly was to live. Pat opened the sty door and Roly trotted in without hesitation. His new surroundings and his companion – a piglet from his own litter – occupied his attention straight away, to the exclusion of everything else.

We waited a while, chatting, Pat hoping that Roly might spare her a glance. But the friendly little pig had returned where he belonged, he paid no attention to what was happening outside his sty – which was just as it should be. She murmured as we turned and walked away, 'I'm glad he's settled down so quickly . . .'

147

But that night, as we were sorting all our various beasties and birds into their sleeping quarters – and ourselves into our own – Pat paused a minute and said thoughtfully, 'Well, Roly's got his own sort of company tonight . . . but I wonder if he'll think about his hot water bottle and his blanket . . .

A little while later we had another animal of a different kind, and this came from Belle Vue.

Two elderly Barbary sheep had mated and produced twins, which I understand in itself is unusual, in addition to the parents being beyond the age where they normally produce young. The twins were weaklings, one died straight away and the other one was abandoned by its mother. This survivor, a poor little creature, was taken into the dispensary and bottle-fed. We saw her, and we should have left her there – but, of course, we didn't.

Peter didn't hold out much hope for her. She'd been born too late, out in the wild she'd have died, like her twin; hand-reared she still didn't stand much chance. 'She's a weird little thing,' he said, which was true. But to Pat she was another small animal that needed caring for.

'I think she's lovely,' she said.

Peter picked up the lamb and plonked it in her arms. 'Well, you'd better take her.'

Even if she'd been inclined to refuse, Pat couldn't then.

So Twinkle, five days old, came home tucked under Pat's arm. She was bottle fed on a mixture of evaporated and steri-lised milk and she grew, very slowly, which was probably just as well because a healthy Barbary sheep grows to make quite a big animal. She wanted food constantly and followed Pat every-where, making a funny little bleating noise. Intake has to have an output, although in Twinkle's case the two seemed unrela-ted, as her puddles were never-ending and Pat was kept mop-ping up after her all day long.

During the day she was in the kitchen. She took to the cats without the least trouble; living with them, she acted like them and was made a fuss of and carried about, just as they were. She had a box in the bedroom where she was supposed to sleep and for a little while she allowed herself to be tucked up at night and stayed where she was put.

As her rickety legs strengthened she grew adventurous and we found that it wasn't necessary to pick her up to put her on the settee or an armchair, she could climb up by herself. That, however, was the limit of her enterprise, she could get up but not down and she very soon learned that if she just stood and bleated we'd pick her up and put her on the floor.

Once she started climbing she did it everywhere and one night she got out of her box and climbed on the bed. There were a couple of cats there so I suppose she couldn't see what objection there would be to her joining them.

'My God, a sheep. What next?' Pat muttered. 'Oh, you might as well let her stay, otherwise we'll only spend the rest of the night putting her back in her box . . .'

Poor Twinkle was a pretty creature, but her intelligence didn't develop to match her agility. There was a terrible noise one night, clatterings and scraping and gruntings, and Pat and I lay in what I can only call a state of hysterical disbelief, listening. We knew exactly where the noise was coming from; Twinkle had got her bearings completely wrong. At last Pat said it — 'She's climbed on the bloody dressing table.'

'Yes. Perhaps . . .' we were whispering, trying to stifle our laughter. 'Perhaps she'll get down by herself.'

'Does she *ever*?'

No, not Twinkle. A minute later she began to bleat, a thin, persistent sound that wore down all our attempts to ignore it. I got up that time to take her off the dressing table, a few nights later it was Pat's turn — then mine — then we knew we wouldn't be able to keep it up indefinitely. We couldn't leave Twinkle in the kitchen at night, she'd only come up the stairs, looking for us, she knew the way well enough, she followed Pat up regularly every day and had to be carried down again. So we put Twinkle in her box in the bathroom.

'It's best, really,' Pat said. 'Because she'll have to go back to the zoo eventually. As soon as she learns to feed herself.'

But for once Pat wasn't looking at things as they really were, and neither was I. We hadn't from the beginning. Twinkle was one of nature's rejects, she'd been born to parents that were too old to produce a lamb fit to survive, and they knew best – they'd rejected her. She never learned to eat by herself no matter how much we encouraged her, and she passed, very quickly, from the juvenile stage to a premature senility and died suddenly, only four months old.

'We'll know better next time. We'll be sensible,' Pat said.

Will we? I hope so.

Fifteen

Hawk and dove

Pinkie, the collared dove, had been in the claws of a cat. She arrived badly cut, her tail feathers gone, one leg deeply bitten. I cleaned her up, washed her wounds with disinfectant, treated them with antibiotic powder and put her by herself in the front room. As I've said, I found that the way to ensure all the animals lived in harmony was to introduce any newcomer, on arrival, to the residents, but I thought that in this case it was best to defer the introductions. The dove had seen one cat too many: to suddenly find itself sharing living quarters with three wasn't guaranteed to aid its recovery. I decided it was best left to itself for a while.

Pinkie's scars healed and her tail began to look more respectably like a tail – but she wasn't destined to keep it that way for very long. The young kestrels, straying into the front room, discovered her there one day and began a game of tweaking her tail feathers. When they went away she followed them. She didn't fly – there was nothing wrong with her wings, she just preferred to walk, pattering out of the front room into the tiny hall. The curtain that hung between the hall and the kitchen was drawn back; Pinkie went on walking, through the opening, into the kitchen.

Jeannie was on the perch directly over the kitchen door; the cats were disposed – as usual with extreme comfort – before the fire. They stirred lazily and looked at the dove without much interest, she was a strange bird – but she was just another bird.

Pinkie's previous encounter with a cat had obviously taught her nothing at all. Unperturbed, she took herself on a tour of inspection, walking about between chair legs, round the side-board, under the television to the corner where the stairs were and the curtain hung across the scullery entrance. She turned back there, pattered along by the cage under the stairs where the mynah birds were, on to the carpet and finally halting in the middle of the kitchen, standing and looking about with bright, busy interest, watched by the three cats and by Jeannie from her perch.

The young kestrels, obviously regarding her as some kind of target practice, started to dive on her again, clouting her tail. Pinkie had had quite enough of that. She scampered, eluding them, then finally took to the air herself, flying up and perching beside Jeannie.

I'd watched all this, amazed at the boldness of the dove who, dispensing with my assistance, had made her own intro-ductions. But Jeannie could be another matter . . . I had a twist of apprehension wondering if – startled and presented with a delicious little stranger – she might not suddenly answer the latent promptings of her nature and make a dinner of it.

But Jeannie's hunting instinct had never developed, or, if it had, it had been deflected into the searching out and picking up of objects, one of her favourite pastimes. Anything on the floor fascinated her, the smallest piece of cotton, an elastic band, a ball of wool, a scrap of paper. Finding something, she'd pick it up delicately in her beak and walk about with it for a long time, occasionally putting it down to examine it, then picking it up again.

Pinkie, landing beside her, studied her, her head twisted round to look up at the big, puzzled hawk. Finding her own mysterious assurance, she sidled along the perch until her soft body touched one of Jeannie's legs. Jeannie drew herself up, uttering a faint squeak of indignation. Undeterred, the dove ex-amined the enormous spread of the talons clutching the perch, dipping her head and making gently exploratory pecks at them. Jeannie squeaked again, louder, indignant, but the dove ignored her.

'Perhaps she's deaf,' I said to Pat, who had come to watch.

'She's daft,' Pat said.

'Yes . . . but whatever she is, she's safe enough.'

And she was, and seemed to know it. After that she spent most of her days in the front room; but in the evenings the pattering of her claws could be heard outside in the hall and Pat would say, 'Lift the curtain. Here she comes, visiting . . .' And dignified and charming, like some plump little royal personage, Pinkie would make her entrance, walking in to spend the evening with her friends.

Determined to get the attention due to her, she took to approaching the cats one after another until eventually Dinah gave in. They took it in turns to chase each other, conducting a sedate game of tag under the chairs – Dinah patting Pinkie's tail, turning and slinking away while Pinkie rushed after her, pecking at *her* tail. After a while Dinah, growing bored, went back to her place by the fire and it was time for the rougher stuff. The boisterous kestrels took over, hurtling about the kitchen, diving to grab at Pinki's tail; when she'd had enough of that she hid under a chair or took herself up to perch beside Jeannie.

Jeannie was very longsuffering with Pinkie, just how longsuffering I realised when I looked up one evening and saw that Pinkie was not beside Jeannie – she was underneath her. Underneath . . . perched between the massive claws of the hawk and pecking away at the long legs until they shifted fractionally, outwards, making room for the dove to settle herself comfortably.

I stared up. 'How did she get *there*?'

'Well, perhaps Jeannie had her foot in her pocket . . .' Pat suggested, '. . . and Pinkie just sort of sidled along.'

Jeannie, like most birds, had a habit of standing on one leg; the other leg she drew up, claw clenched and tucked into her feathers; we called it putting her foot in her pocket. But we never found out if this was how the dove got under Jeannie, because we never saw her do it. We saw her pecking away at Jeannie's legs until she had them exactly the right distance apart; we saw her wriggling and fidgeting, making herself comfortable; we saw Jeannie's body slowly descend on her until only a tiny beak was visible . . . sometimes we never saw anything at all and went and reached up to the perch, feeling about underneath Jeannie until we found the dove.

Often Jeannie was visibly and utterly fed-up; she would make herself go very tall and lean back slightly, her head going square with annoyance. But she never flew away or attempted to do anything *positive*; she just went on sitting, looking disgruntled, with Pinkie peeping out from underneath her with all the implacable sweetness of an old lady who has taken the best seat by the fire and doesn't intend giving it up for anyone.

Pinkie died very suddenly one evening. Pat stepped over Dinah and the dove as they dodged about playing their game of tag; she went into the scullery for a few moments and when she came out Pinkie was lying on the floor.

She had died as swiftly as the blinking of an eyelid, probably her heart had just given out. There was a very slight scratch on her, scarcely detectable, nothing like the wounds she had been suffering from when she arrived; so obviously Dinah could not be held responsible for her death.

For several days the Siamese cat searched for her playmate, sniffing around the kitchen and the empty front room. Jeannie didn't appear to miss her – or, if she did, I maintain it was with relief, having regained her perch and her dignity and no longer being nagged, pecked and conned into acting as tea-cosy to a dove.

At last Jeannie got her full plumage, and she was a beautiful bird. Her overall colour was a reddish bronze with subtle gradations and interminglings of shade from the pale sorrel of her chest to the fiery russet of her body; her wings darkening outwards to the edging of primary feathers and tips of the secondaries of a sable so deep as to be almost black; the deep sable repeated in a fine collar of feathers round her neck. Above the collar her face was pale with an ivory delicacy in which her nutbrown eyes glowed; her legs were creamy coloured, heavily scaled, her claws jet. She stood almost eighteen inches tall and her wing-span just reached four feet.

Pat opened a book one day and there was a picture of the bird who, across the kitchen, was perched on the back of my chair: a Busarellus Nigricollis, a South American fishing hawk, sometimes called the black-collared hawk. Her natural home was southern and central America; she had certainly come a long way, had Jeannie.

In her wild state she could have lived on fish; knowing this was the natural diet of a bird of her type, we had already tried to feed it to her. On each occasion she had tasted it and spat it out. She had grown accustomed to the meat she had been reared on and had no intention of changing to anything else.

Having been handled, virtually as far back as her memory could go, she had no fear at all of human beings. Almost obsessively affectionate with us, she was also very friendly with anyone who might call. When an inquisitive, amiable, full grown hawk lands on a visitor's knee a little reassurance is necessary – the kind of reassurance offered by the owners of large, boisterous dogs – 'It's all right, don't be alarmed, she won't hurt you . . .'

And she was a very gentle bird indeed; if she ever did any damage it was through clumsiness, that was all, and she was good-tempered, at times very longsuffering, with the other birds. She would let Pat do anything: feed her, tease her, carry her about, take her into the yard for her bath; and it was because Pat had absolutely no doubts about how she would behave that she agreed at once with me when I suggested, 'Let's take Jeannie for a walk.'

Taking the birds for a walk was something that I did regularly. Perdita, when she was not working, needed fresh air, and that was how she got it. By then I had become a member of the British Falconer's Club, and I'd acquired another buzzard.

This second buzzard was called Horus – mistakenly, because she was a female, but she already had her name when I bought her and it stuck. She was young and untrained and her physical condition was poor, so she needed to be treated carefully to be brought to the fitness necessary for flying. I took her out on my fist as part of the initial stage of her training, just as I'd done with Perdita. She was a neatly built, goodlooking bird, smaller

155

than Perdita and by temperament much less aggressive. Pat often carried her when we went out for a spot of fresh air, while I carried Perdita. If Pat was busy, I'd take one buzzard out for its walk, come back, return it to its perch and take the other one out.

On this particular evening, when it was Perdita's turn to go out, I suggested we take Jeannie along for company. Pat was the one who carried her, and she wore a heavy glove; Jeannie's claws were a tremendous size, they could completely encircle Pat's wrist. Docile and affectionate as she was, there was always the possibility that something outdoors might startle her, causing her to grip her 'perch' defensively, and as her perch was flesh and bone the dagger-like talons would make a terrible mess of it.

The streets were quiet, the air mild with a hint of approaching summer. People locally had long since ceased to react to the sight of us taking our constitutional accompanied by birds; occasionally someone would wave, or stop for a word and pass by.

Jeannie was completely composed, it didn't matter much to her where she was, so long as she was with Pat. Previously, all she had known of the world was what she had seen of it from the bedroom window. To be carried about outdoors amongst unfamiliar sights and sounds occasioned her no alarm, and very little interest; most of her attention was taken up in studying first Pat, then me, then Perdita, then Pat again. When she did look around it was in a rather indifferent manner, and only at what was on a level with her, she didn't look up at the sky. She'd never flown outdoors, possible she didn't comprehend that that was what outdoors was *for*; her flying was done in the house, her world was the house, this unexpected episode was incidental, time out from the routine of her days.

Pat was intrigued by Jeannie's manner and noticed her slightest reaction – not that there was a great deal to notice until a dog ran up to us. The dog pranced about, jumping up, eager to examine the strange creatures carried by the human beings. Perdita squawked abuse at him, she didn't like anything very much and she particularly didn't like dogs.

156

Horus, a European Buzzard

A heron on the back porch

(*above*) Pat holding Barny the owl while Bob holds Kit a kestrel. (*below, left to right*) Pat with Horus; a friend with Jeannie; Bob with Perdita. This photograph was taken in 1972

Perdita, a European Buzzard

Jeannie, perplexed, sidled up Pat's arm as far as the esses would allow. Peering down at the dog she drew herself up on her long legs, elongating her body until she was incredib y tall and thin; then she inclined herself sideways until she was leaning against Pat. From the security of that position she squeaked, pesteringly, until I shoo'd the dog away.

We didn't stay out very long. Pat knew from experience how light a bird felt on the fist initially and how, in a surprisingly short space of time, its weight seemed to increase out of all proportion to its size, and Jeannie was a big bird. At first, Pat held her arm away from her body in the correct manner; but as her arm began to ache, and Jeannie grew heavier, she drew her arm in to ease the strain. Jeannie, taking advantage of this closeness, leaned against Pat, occasionally giving a soft, contented squeak.

'It's all right for you, you daft thing,' Pat said gently to her.

'Bob . . . I think my arm's breaking.'

'OK Trish, we'll go back now, shall we?'

So we went home, after taking Jeannie on her first walk down the street to the clay pit; retracing our steps, walking and talking quietly in the mild evening air, with Perdita brooding grandly in her sublime, self-contained way on my fist and Jeannie leaning against Pat.

One evening we went out a little later than usual and it was dusk as we began the return journey. In the street we paused to speak to a neighbour and Pat noticed a faint restlessness steal over Jeannie. Forgetting to speak or listen, she watched her.

The bird fidgeted, hesitantly turning her head this way and that, Leaning out and sideways from Pat's arm she craned to see something, even peeping over Pat's shoulder. Pat looked about, trying to work out what it was that had, at last, roused Jeannie's interest. At first she didn't understand then, following the direction of the slowly weaving, fascinated gaze, she saw that Jeannie was examining the street lamps.

She had never seen them before; she had never been out in the dark when they'd been lit and never looked at them from the window. They took her attention as nothing outdoors had ever done, like so many small moons strung out along the street, glimmering away into the enfolding darkness; and she looked at them from left to right, very slowly, then back again, one by one – as if she was counting them.

When he was flying, Kit lived on a perch upstairs in the house; when he was moulting, or resting, he lived in the aviary. Keeping an eye on him, I noticed that he was looking a little frail, a little scruffy. I waited for him to get his new plumage after a moult, thinking that this would smarten him up. But it didn't, and I had to accept things as they were: time had passed and worked its change on the alert, dapper little kestrel; Kit was old, he had to be retired.

I couldn't bear to leave him in the aviary, subject to changes of weather, competing with the younger birds for his food until he was too exhausted to fend for himself. I brought him in the house where, after all the service and pleasure he had given, he would in return be comfortable and cared for.

Kit ate the food that was given to him; he didn't fly very much and chose his own, quiet places to perch. Once or twice, when he flew, he would dip suddenly to the floor or the seat of a chair and lurch and flutter about, his wings outspread. After scarcely a minute he would give his body a shake, as if to pull himself together, and go on his way.

One day he half fluttered, half flopped to the floor. His wings were stretched out, wide open and rigid. He gave a strange little cry and pitched forward, his body turning again and again in terrible, involuntary spasms. I dived for him, caught him, and held him, feeling the twitch and jerk of the muscles. After about a couple of minutes the seizure passed and I gently put Kit down. In a little while he was fluttering about, then flying to his favourite perch to settle there.

A few days later he had another fit. This one was longer and it took him longer to recover from it. When he did, I could see how rapidly his faculties were becoming impaired. Then the third fit came, following too closely on the second, and it was very severe.

Pat picked up the kestrel immediately the fit started – the

158

strange, lost little cry had warned her it was about to happen. We had a visitor in the kitchen at the time; Pat murmured to me that she would take Kit upstairs, out of the way, where it was dark and quiet – just as, at one time, she had taken Jeannie into the dark hall during her fits.

Upstairs, she knew she must make the decision I hadn't been able to make. The kestrel was old and tired, she wouldn't see his frail body racked needlessly, without hope of recovery. She came to the top of the stairs to tell me to bring the ether. She didn't need to call me, I'd been waiting, on edge, half in and half out of the kitchen. She just said, 'Bob –' and I answered, 'Yes?' But on the instant we spoke she felt every scrap of tension leave the kestrel's body, its small frame lost shape in a sudden limpness, its head lolled to one side.

'Nothing,' Pat said quietly. 'It doesn't matter now . . .' Kit, our first and best loved kestrel, had died lying in her hand.

Sixteen

Medusa

I answered the door one night to a family who were on their way home from a holiday in Scotland. They had with them a bundle about the size of a very large hen stitched up in a towel; as they handed it over they told Pat and me the story of how they had come by it and, in consequence, found their way to us.

They were keen fishermen and one day towards the end of their holiday they found a dead bird lying on the ground at the side of the road; at least, as it was completely inert they took it to be dead. There was a suggestion that its feathers would be just the thing for fly-tying and on a general agreement someone went to pluck one out. The bird moved.

Realising that after all there was life in it and it could possibly be helped, they found a vet who unfortunately would not treat it. The family then took the bird to the local police, explaining that they had by then finished their holiday and were about to return to Lancashire. 'In that case,' the policeman said, 'if you're travelling to England there's a bird man somewhere near Manchester. He'll take it off you and look after it.' He could supply no more details about locating the 'bird man'. The family, on arriving in Manchester, thought of referring to Belle Vue as a possible source of information; they telephoned there and were sent on to us.

The bird they had with them hadn't been fed. This was not unkindness, no one knew what on earth to give it. It had been wrapped and stitched into the towel to prevent it doing any further damage to itself, and placed in a box. When I heard it had been like this for four days I thought that – although all the actions of the family had been intended for the best – I would find a very dispirited bird indeed; it was a wonder to me it hadn't died of heat prostration. But the bird that emerged from its wrappings proved to have all the toughness and fury of its kind, one that I recognised at once – a young European buzzard. Its right leg was broken high up at the thigh, it had probably flown into something – a car, perhaps, as it had been found beside the road – and was still in a stunned state when the family found it.

Having done as much as they could, the family said goodbye to us and left. It was good luck that shortly afterwards two of the keepers from Belle Vue happened to call by on a visit because, injured and hungry though the bird was, it took four of us to deal with it while the necessary first aid was carried out. Its beak and the claw of its good leg were razor sharp and it lashed out with them, squawking and struggling. While the two keepers held it I set the break and tried to keep the leg in place and Pat applied the plaster of Paris bandage. This set in a matter of seconds and I then looked at the rest of the buzzard as best I could. The right wing was dropped, there was an abscess on the shoulder that was at bursting point, in fact it did burst as I was examining it, so I cleaned it up and treated it with ointment.

After that we fed it and set it on the back of a chair. It stayed there for days, a young, bewildered bird, its bad wing and the weight of the plaster on its leg effectively preventing it from moving about. As it perched there the glare it levelled on anyone who approached it was so intimidating it made me say, 'That stare's enough to turn you to stone.' For this reason I called the buzzard Medusa, taking it to be a female. The classical association was correct but the gender was wrong, and by the time I realised my mistake the name had stuck and later caused considerable confusion.

Medusa's disablement did nothing to improve his temper. He ate greedily and savagely – it took two of us to feed him as he was – literally – inclined to take lumps out of the nearest thing. One evening, when we'd had him for a couple of days, the telephone rang as we were feeding him. Pat said, 'It's sure to be for you, go ahead. I'll manage . . .'

Her confidence was for once misplaced. During the course of

the call she allowed her attention to be distracted momentarily by something I was saying. A split second was enough for Medusa. Supported on his plaster of Paris cast, he lashed out with his good claw and snatched Pat's hand. It was done so quickly Pat couldn't at once take in what had happened. Shock briefly drove away all sensation of pain, all she could comprehend was that she was standing in the kitchen with an enraged buzzard clamped to her. Then the pain and the blood welled up together and she realised that the buzzard's front and hind tces were bedded so deeply in her hand the claws must have been close to meeting.

She said, 'Bob . . .' weakly – too weakly to alarm me because I finished my phone call, assuming that the bird had been misbehaving, as usual, and the sound Pat made had been telling him off. Then I put the receiver down and turned round and saw that the bird was attached to her – and saw *how* it was attached . . . It took quite some time to prise the claws free and clean and dress the two holes they'd left in Pat's hand. The wound gave her a great deal of trouble, as well as inconvenience, for days, during which she and Medusa eyed each other's bandaged limbs with equal disenchantment.

While the cast was still on the bird began to lumber about, flying and landing with great clumsiness but nevertheless showing the will to try his wings. He ignored the cats and the other birds; like Perdita he was a brooder, a loner, anti more or less everything.

After six weeks I decided the cast should come off. The leg had had the right length of time to heal and if it hadn't done so by then it never would. If we had a fight to get it on we had just as much difficulty getting it off, and this time there were only the two of us to manage. The only practical way – and the method by which we hoped to escape with minimum injuries – was to wrap the bird in a towel, leaving the right leg free. Medusa thought this was a rotten idea and in spite of being half mummified put up an enormous amount of resistance, but at last we got him on the table, Pat holding him while I cut through the plaster with strong scissors. As soon as it was off we unrolled the towel and leapt clear. Medusa flounced himself upright, gave us a malevolent glare, found himself suddenly free of the encumbering weight and shot upwards in what was practically a vertical take-off.

I was dissatisfied with the mended leg. It had the very slightest kink in it but there was nothing I could do about that. If the bird hadn't been such a terrible patient in the first place (no one expected him to cooperate but at least he could have resigned himself) he would have had a perfectly straight leg at the end of it all. The leg gave him no trouble but the fact that it was slightly bent, plus the persistently dropped wing, meant that Medusa's flight and agility were impaired, and in the wild he wouldn't be equal to the task of caring for himself. We kept him in the house for a while, to make sure everything was all right, then he was put into the aviary in the yard with some kestrels and Horus, the other buzzard.

It was springtime, a softening of the harsh air and an imperceptible sense of things growing, beginning. When Pat went out into the yard one morning her attention was attracted by a series of soft little squeaks. Wondering what could be the cause of the sound she looked into the aviary and saw Horus sitting on the ground, her tail up in the air, piping this absurd little song – the significance of which didn't at that moment occur to Pat.

After a couple of days of this unlikely behaviour Pat thought to mention it to me. When I saw the big bird cuddled up and twittering away – rather like a singing tea-cosy – I also noticed Medusa, on his perch, eyeing her with a wealth of understanding and intent. Mythologically misnamed they might be, the buzzards could still be relied on to get their roles right. 'They're mating,' I said to Pat, and sure enough, very shortly afterwards, the two buzzards began industriously building a nest.

We waited with interest and excitement to see if anything would come of this, as buzzards usually only mate when in their wild state. One day Pat went into the aviary where Horus was sitting on the nest. The buzzard showed no sign of hostility, in fact she obligingly stood up for a moment and allowed Pat a

164

glimpse of her one egg. Pat took to visiting her regularly; two days later the performance was repeated – this time there were two eggs. Over a space of eight days Horus laid four eggs, then settled down to hatch them.

Although she had no objection to Pat's presence and would let her go right up to the nest, the buzzard wouldn't allow me any closer than a couple of feet. An invisible demarcation line marked out the limit acceptable to Horus, if I attempted to cross it she would mantle and glare, warning me off.

But the excitement and the waiting came to nothing, after all. Pat went into the aviary on her regular daily visit, knowing that the incubation period was almost over, and found that the eggs had gone. Disappointed, she told me when I came home. I went out glumly to have a look but could find no trace of the eggs. I could only conclude that the buzzard herself had smashed and eaten them. What mysterious force of nature moved in her no one could tell, perhaps some defect in the eggs prompted her to destroy them.

Both birds used the nest after that, to make themselves comfortable in when the mood took them. It is still there in the aviary, so are the buzzards and, as Pat often hopefully observes, there's always another spring . . .

In the grounds of a nearby school three baby magpies were blown from their nest in a tall tree. They were picked up by a boy who saw that one had died straight away. The tree was much too tall for him to climb to return the other two; somehow he got hold of our address and brought them here and handed them over – two bald splodges of skin the size of hen's eggs, with wide open beaks.

Pat fed them by the same method she had fed Tich, a hypodermic syringe fitted with a bicycle valve rubber, pumping the food into their funny skin-and-bone bodies and tucking them up together in an old blackbird's nest that had been brought to us once, complete with newly-hatched birds that unfortunately hadn't survived. We put the nest in a cardboard box to guard against draughts and the possibility of the birds falling out, and that night the box was put on top of the freezer so that they could have the muted vibration of the motor for company. For one, however, this care was wasted – when I looked in the box in the morning only one magpie had survived.

Once, long before, we'd looked after a magpie that had been brought to us from Eccles; we'd called him Eccles then and in memory of him we called the new one by the same name. He became a clown, a thief, a chattering trickster; going through the absurd stage of growing his feathers, a ridiculous little bundle of down and spikes; teaching himself to fly with an exuberant disregard for anyone or anything in his way; teasing the kestrels and the cats, daring to tweak the buzzards' feathers as he flew past – I was aghast at this, no bird in its right mind will tweak a buzzard, but Eccles was too cheeky to care about anyone's dignity – or temper.

He grew to be a big, handsome bird, and in the process he began to steal. Anything. It is often said that magpies are attracted to objects only because they glitter, for Eccles it didn't matter whether a thing glittered or not – if it was movable, it was his.

He started in a small way – a scrap of paper here, a hairgrip there. Pat grew accustomed to finding a variety of objects on top of the bookcase and either throwing them away or returning them to their rightful places; it was, she thought philosophically, just the way of magpies. Then she missed an earring and hunted unavailingly for it. A little later another earring – from a different pair – disappeared. She realised we were going to have to take extra care with anything we valued.

'That magpie's getting to be an absolute menace,' she complained to me.

'It's just his way,' I said, adopting an attitude of forbearance that disintegrated later into oaths when I drew the curtains and was bombarded by an assortment of ball-point pens, plastic teaspoons, scraps of paper and matchboxes that Eccles, in an orgy of pilfering, had tucked into the folds of the curtain.

After that, in the hope of discouraging him, we took to shouting 'Stop it!' when we caught him on the wing, bearing away loot. When he was in the mood he obeyed, swooping down and releasing whatever he carried in a simple dive-bombing tactic – it was inevitable that when he began to talk the first words he ever said were, 'Stop it!'

One day Pat missed a ring she had taken off and placed on a shelf while she was washing her hands; there was no doubt about who had taken it, the question was *where had he put it?* She searched all his hiding places, well aware that there were many more no one knew anything about, but she couldn't find the ring. Later though, she did, and although it was too much to hope that some dim awareness of the principles of ownership stirred in the magpie's mind, it was odd that she should come upon it hidden in her own knitting basket.

One evening we went out for a few hours. When we returned and stepped into the kitchen, switching on the light, we were presented with a spectacle of such disorder we stood for a moment speechless. Thoughts of burglars and vandals occupied us only fleetingly, there was nothing missing, no destruction and not *quite* enough mess. The muddle was random, childlike . . . birdlike . . . 'It's that magpie,' Pat yelled. Who else but the magpie would have pattered along every flat surface pushing on to the floor every object that lay in its path?

It couldn't go on. Once the magpie had discovered such a fascinating game it was probable he would play it every minute he was unattended, and with his stealing, his teasing of the kestrels and cats, he was becoming too much of a nuisance altogether. We decided to put him in the extension for a while, where he could do whatever he liked and no one would suffer the consequences.

It was summer when we put him there. One day Pat went into the yard and left the door of the extension open. There was a whirl of wings, a swoop, and with a flash of his beautiful iridiscent feathers, Eccles made his break for freedom.

He was out of sight in a moment. 'Well, that's it,' Pat thought. He was fit and strong, only a very young bird but well able to take care of himself, so his chances of survival were very good indeed. She came and told me – I happened to be home because it was Saturday – 'Eccles has flown away. Gone. Fled.'

'That's a relief,' I said. 'He was driving me mad.'

In the nature of the life we lead one bird can be replaced, within minutes, by another. Less than an hour after Eccles had flown off a neighbour called in. 'Can you come round quickly and do something?' she asked me. 'Mrs G – is a bit nervous, there's a mynah bird got into her house.'

The weather was hot and everyone had their doors and windows open. As I hurried off I thought to myself that the mynah must obviously be somebody's strayed pet, so accustomed to the company of human beings it had to find somebody to attach itself to. I wondered who in the locality had lost a mynah and if there was some way of finding out and restoring the bird to its owner.

I could have saved myself the mental exercise. The bird wasn't a mynah at all, it was the errant Eccles, greeting me with a chatter of recognition and swooping on to my shoulder. 'You didn't get far, did you?' I muttered accusingly as we made our way home.

'Stop it!' Eccles shouted joyfully.

'That is *not* a mynah bird,' Pat greeted us when we walked in.

'I know. It's Eccles pretending to be a mynah,' I answered. 'This bird is capable of anything.'

But we knew that what had happened was what we most deplored: for once unmindful of the consequences, we'd brought up a wild thing as a pet, the intelligent and companionable magpie was now too tame to seek his natural environment.

In proof of this, Eccles never made another attempt to fly away. It didn't matter how often Pat deliberately let the door of the extension stand open as she went in and out, how often she muttered, '*Some* people get to *know* when they're not wanted.' Eccles wasn't going anywhere.

When I had any work to do in the yard, the magpie accompanied me, perching on the nearest convenient spot and keeping me in sight. His vocabulary had extended from his favourite 'Stop it!' to 'What are you doin?' and 'Will you shut up?' One day out in the yard with me he attempted a lengthier sentence but I couldn't make out what it was. I called in to Pat,

'This bird's trying to say something. I can't tell what it is.'

Pat was busy in the house. She had to leave what she was doing and come outside, saying with exasperation to me, 'What *are* you going on about?'

'What *are* you going on about?' the magpie repeated, clearly mimicking Pat's scolding tone.

'That was it,' I said, subsiding. I had two of them to nag me now.

After he'd been in the extension a short while the enterprising magpie discovered the cat-flap at the bottom of the door; this led into the scullery and from there to the kitchen. Once he realised the freedom of the house was his whenever he felt inclined to enjoy it – and that was ninety-nine percent of the time – he couldn't be persuaded to stay out, and his antics made him less than welcome. So it was the aviary for Eccles.

He had plenty to occupy him there, terrorising the kestrels and teasing the buzzards. The big birds could look after themselves, but when Pat saw the much smaller kestrels being bullied too much she would shoot into the aviary and swat Eccles away. After a couple of buffetings Eccles learned how to outwit her; he dived straight into the box where the hedgehogs slept and waited safely amongst their prickles until she'd gone away.

His habit of tweaking the buzzards' feathers finally landed him in trouble. When Horus and Medusa were nest-building they were too touchy to put up with his clowning. Pat heard a screech one day and ran to the door of the extension, and from there she could see that Medusa had got Eccles. The buzzard must have grabbed him just as he was flying past and caught him by the rear end. One foot on his perch, the other grasping the magpie – holding him upright as if he was an iced lolly – Medusa eyed his prize with evil satisfaction.

It was pouring with rain. From the shelter of the extension Pat shouted, 'Put that bird down –' But Medusa ignored her and just went on holding the screeching magpie, who was going at top speed through a garbled version of his entire vocabulary.

Getting wetter by the minute, Pat went to let herself into the aviary. She had suffered at Medusa's claws herself and knew

169

that she was going to have a battle to remove Eccles from them. The iron grip was likely to squeeze the life out of him. A battle and perhaps a few scars herself . . . an unpleasant prospect, but Pat didn't pause to consider it. She was angry with the buzzard, the magpie, the rain – everything. Putting all the unconscious force of her authority into her command she said again, '*Put that bird down.*'

Medusa turned to look at her, watching her closing in. He knew – they all knew – who was most *likely* to be boss when it came to the final count. With a gesture of comprehensive disgust he flung the magpie at her.

Eccles landed in a puddle. Pat picked him up, soaked, dazed but unharmed, and took him into the extension until he recovered. Then she gave him a talking-to (for all the good that would do) and put him back in the aviary. Eccles had learned one lesson the hard way; he left the buzzards alone after that.

Seventeen

A few ducks . . . and some geese

One day when we were driving past our local park we caught sight of an acquaintance coming out of the park gates. As soon as he saw us the man stepped off the pavement and waved us down. 'I'm glad I've seen you. I was coming round to tell you – one of your ducks is loose in the park.'

At that time I didn't have any ducks, and said so; but, naturally, being interested I prepared to get out of the car and go and have a look. Before I could do so, the duck appeared. It walked out of the park, crossed the pavement and set off down the road in the most leisurely and unconcerned manner.

I recognised it at once as a sheld-duck, conspicuously attractive with its dark green, chestnut and white plumage. I got out of the car and with my friend began to follow it.

At first the duck took no notice, but when we began to close in it quickened its pace and led us in and out of gardens, across roads and down alleyways for almost half an hour before we managed to catch it. I tucked it under my arm and went back to the car where Pat was waiting and wondering just how many people in the neighbourhood had been diverted by the sight of two large men chasing a pretty and determined little duck.

We took it home and had a look at it. One of its eyes was rather messy but as it was impossible to tell what sort of damage it had suffered we could only bathe it and treat it with ointment. After the duck had been in the aviary a little while it was obvious the medication had had the right result; with the duck perfectly fit and the aviary crowded, we had to look round for a new home for it.

We found the ideal one with a friend who had a flight pool on his land near Southport. The attractive little wanderer was taken there, put amongst assorted water birds to settle – as far as we were concerned – happily ever after.

But the duck, as we later learnt, had a mind of its own. After a short while it was missing from the pool; my friend, Ken, wondered where it could have got to and within a few days he found out. He was approached by a neighbour, a lady who lived further down the road and had an ornamental duck pond. 'You'll never guess what's come to live in my pond,' she said, in great excitement.

'I've got a pretty good idea,' Ken answered. And sure enough, it was the sheld-duck. Having turned up in Manchester (we never found out from whence) and been taken to Southport, it had decided to choose its own home and to the delight of its new owner settled down as a decorative resident amongst the other ducks.

The next duck was a Muscovy, brought to us with a broken wing. In spite of its injuries it was a good-natured creature, accepting our ministrations with docility. A plaster cast, of the same type used for Medusa's leg, wasn't suitable on its own and we had to add a splint.

A duck waddling about with its wing in a sling has a comic improbability, appreciated by onlookers but not by the duck itself. Out in the aviary, lugging this weighty encumbrance about, the duck grew markedly morose. I recognised its dejection and sympathised. Determined to try anything to cheer the creature up I dropped round to Peter and asked to borrow one of the zoo's male Muscovies.

'Don't you think there's enough in the way of feathers out there in that yard?' Pat asked, when I arrived home with it under my arm.

'I've only *borrowed* him, just as a bit of company for her. Brighten her up.'

'It'll do more than that if he's got Intentions,' Pat said. 'She's not got much chance of skipping out of the way with that damn great cast on her wing.'

But I was right. In a very short space of time the duck

displayed a noticeably cheerful change of manner and her male companion took kindly to his new surroundings.

In the aviary was an old forty gallon beer barrel. I'd acquired it – empty – and being prepared to make use of anything that came my way, had put it on its side, propping it to keep it from rolling about – a ready-made shelter for any birds that might want to take advantage of it.

And Pat was right, too. The contented duck, her wing healed, went to roost in the barrel.

She nested towards the front of it at first and there she laid a few eggs. After a while she moved her prospective family farther back into the barrel and added to it. After that she moved again, right to the back, and stayed there for about three weeks.

One morning after I'd gone to work and Pat was in the aviary, sounds of activity from the beer barrel attracted her attention. As she watched, the proud mother waddled from the barrel followed by her enchanting brood: one, two, three . . . six . . . nine . . . ten . . . Pat lost count, delighted by the sight of the chicks, fluffy as bumble bees, pattering and scrambling and pecking about the aviary. 'They're *gorgeous*,' she said to herself, wishing I was there to share them with her. But, practical as always, she didn't linger to admire them but set about providing them with water, improvising a pond by turning a dustbin lid upside down and filling it with the hose pipe.

In ones and twos and threes the chicks hopped and splashed into their 'pond', crowding it until there was no room for Mum, who patrolled up and down, keeping a watchful eye on them. Pat counted them, there were thirteen. After their first wetting, and hours spent exploring the world for the first time, the chicks trooped after their mother back into the barrel.

When I came home from work that evening I was greeted with Pat's smiling comment, 'I've just established a new scientific fact. You can actually get thirteen day-old Muscovy chicks on a dustbin lid. Filled with water, of course. You *must* see them.'

But it was days before I saw them. The mother and her chicks were late risers and went early to bed; I had to wait until

Saturday before I could watch the delightful little procession come out for its daily dip. Unfortunately, their numbers had been depleted. The clutch had been a large one – fourteen in all. One egg had never hatched out at all; two of the surviving thirteen, the weaklings, died within the first few days; then one unfortunate ball of down got under its father's large feet.

After that the male Muscovy was returned to Belle Vue, but the ten chicks and their mother stayed for a few weeks, taking up more and more room and making more and more noise until one day, on a routine cleaning out, I said, 'Pat . . . this yard's full of ducks.' 'I wondered when you were going to get round to noticing,' Pat answered. 'Don't you think we ought to do something about it?' So the ducks went, armfuls of them, into the back of the car and off to join their father in Belle Vue.

But, as I said, in the Ratcliffe household space is only made in order to be filled . . .

One evening I had a call from the local RSPCA man who had received reports of two large ducks in trouble on the canal. It was dark and he had only a vague idea where to look – would I go along and help him find them?

I said yes, of course, giving up my quiet evening by the telly and relinquishing my easy chair to assorted cats. 'It shouldn't take long with two of us, and it can't be far,' I said to Pat and went off with the RSPCA official in his van.

In terms of distance it wasn't far, in terms of time it didn't take long, but for mess, discomfort and sheer inconvenience that job established some kind of record. When we'd located the area of the canal where the birds were floundering we found that particular stretch of water to be more than merely clogged: rotted vegetation, debris, effluent and rubbish had accumulated to such a degree the surface of the water had formed a crust that was *just* solid enough to bear the weight of a man. If he ran.

And that was what I did, minus shoes and socks, my trousers rolled up; when I paused in one place too long I started to sink, when I ran too fast my weight drove me through any thinner surfaced spot and I had to flounder out like one of the birds themselves. I kept it up for three quarters of an hour, the equally dedicated (or pitifully misguided, depending on one's viewpoint) RSPCA official for company.

Eventually we caught the birds and took them back home in the van. As far as we knew the birds had been on the canal for several days, local people had been throwing bread to them, which was just as well because there was nothing else but rubbish for them to eat.

In the yard, under the electric light, we set about washing the birds. They were extremely dirty and it would take considerable time and patience to get them into a reasonable state, but as some of the disfiguring mess was removed the two large 'ducks' began to emerge as geese.

One was a Barnacle goose, the other – to my delight – was the rare lesser-white fronted goose. I'd never seen one before but I was familiar with the characteristics and could identify it at once.

The Barnacle goose is not an uncommon bird, but there was no knowing where this could have come from, as the breed is generally confined to coast and marshland. As for the lesser-white front, that was a total mystery. I've heard of them occasionally appearing amongst flocks of the large common white front goose, but then only in the region of the Severn Estuary. At first I thought they'd both escaped from someone's collection, but as they weren't clipped and had no identification marks on them I had to conclude they were wild. A spell of fierce gale winds occurring shortly before the birds turned up on the canal provided the only clue to the appearance of the lesser-white front; to be found in such an unlikely locality must mean that she had been blown in by bad weather.

We kept them both for a while until they were clean and well built up physically, and they certainly added a touch of elegance to the aviary, the tall Barnacle goose with his handsome black and white marks and the lesser-white front, so prettily shaped and coloured she looked like a porcelain ornament.

The next RSPCA call also came at night. Someone had telephoned the police from a factory in Clayton to report that a large bird had got on to the premises and was attacking the night-watchman. The police phoned the RSPCA official who came for me to see if I would lend a hand. As it was so late Pat decided not to go, she was tired and anyway there wasn't a great deal of room in the van. She wasn't in the mood to enjoy being shoved in the back of it with a strange and aggressive bird for company, so she went to bed and we went out.

Locating the factory was easy, getting in proved more difficult. The police had promised to meet us there but as time went by and they didn't appear it was obvious more important matters had turned up to occupy their attention.

We decided we couldn't sit waiting in the van any longer and went to the security men at the main gates and explained who we were and what we were doing there. Someone had forgotten to pass a message on or something and the chaps we spoke to didn't know anything about us. It was by then very late, the factory was working night shift and strangers with wild stories about birds weren't going to be let in to wander about the place willy-nilly. There was a great deal of arguing, cross-checking, examination of whatever identification we could produce; the absence of the police, who were supposed to lend authority to the enterprise, didn't help things along.

At last we were allowed through the gates to begin our search. No one, it seemed, was in the least anxious to accompany us; the unidentified bird had done a fair job of terrorising everyone on the premises. 'I wonder what it *is*?' I murmured, a question that was answered a little later when we saw a shape walking ahead of us up the dimness of the factory's perimeter road. We followed it quickly and stealthily. Unaware of our presence it moved on until it neared the boiler house, then settled itself down near the door. As we drew closer its attention was alerted, it raised itself up and hissing, neck outstretched, began to lumber towards us.

It was a goose, a large female domestic goose and she wasn't in the least aggressive. On the contrary, she'd obviously been treated as a pet and enjoyed the company of people, – this explained her 'attacks' on the night-watchman. Terrifying as her advances were to anyone who didn't know geese, she was just trying to make friends and, I'm willing to bet, she'd probably seen his sandwiches, too.

Thoroughly pleased to have someone take notice of her at last, she let me pick her up and carry her. The security men lurked behind suitable cover and couldn't be persuaded the goose meant no harm. With relief they saw the three of us off the premises, banged the gate resoundingly behind us and returned to their routine.

The goose had no objection to the van when she was put loose in the back. I've found through experience that the big water birds travel best that way, distributing their weight to find their own balance as the van moved along; if they were put in sacks or boxes they become frightened and struggle and run the danger of hurting themselves badly.

When we reached home, in the early hours of the morning, I said goodnight to my friend and carried the goose through the house to the extension. Charles was there – company of a kind, although it was plain he didn't think much of being woken at such an untimely hour. I settled her down with some bread and cabbage leaves and at last went up to bed.

'What is it?' Pat asked sleepily.

'Just an ordinary white goose. I've put it in the extension.'

'Is it all right?'

'Fine. It just wants a roof over its head, that's all.'

'Oh, one of those,' Pat murmured.

It was as well she had some inkling of the goose's disposition. When she went downstairs in the morning, shortly after I'd gone to work, and opened the door of the extension, she was immediately smothered by an affectionate goose, rushing at her with its wings out as if it would envelop her in its embrace.

It was a good-natured creature but its hunger for company was embarrassing. Strong, amiable and in love with any human being who had a kind word for it, it lay in wait for Pat behind the extension door, greeting her ecstatically and trying to follow her back into the house when she left it. This friendliness, though charming, was very wearing, Pat knew she couldn't spend the next few days wrestling with a great deal of goose in order to keep it out of the kitchen. She put it firmly in the yard, hoping that its owner would soon turn up and claim it.

But it seemed that no one wanted to claim it. Over the course of the next three days I asked around the various police stations and RSPCA officials. Some miles away there are several small-holdings bordering the canal, I assumed that the goose had come from one of these and travelled down the canal, which passed through the premises of a great many factories in the industrial area. But no one reported a goose missing, no one made any enquiries about it; so wherever it had come from it was plain it wasn't going back there again.

We couldn't keep her in the yard, as she was too big. She needed space and we were overcrowded – as usual – and an open door was to her an invitation to step inside and make herself at home. Domestic geese don't go in for flying much, although she could have got out of the yard if she had found its confinement irksome. The height of the walls would not in that case have been a deterrent, but she made no attempt to go. Mrs Goose would have to be taken away, somewhere. Anywhere.

We turned to our friend Maggie, who offered a home on her farm at Alderley. There the goose went one Sunday, sitting in the back of the car as comfortably as a large cushion, interested in everything and perfectly content, when she reached her new home, to settle down with so much human and feathered company.

Eighteen

Our own little world

We were accustomed to Jeannie's friendliness, but strangers were often overwhelmed by it. The fishing hawk did have a majestic and possibly fierce look as she perched above the kitchen door, so out of place in such ordinary surroundings, gazing at any visitor with mesmerised interest. Then she would get ready to move in for closer inspection, her head lowering, her body flattening out, the great wings spreading at the moment she launched herself.

The end result of this impressive display was merely an overture of friendship. Jeannie would perch on the back of the chair, gazing down. Encouraged, she would hop down on to the visitor's knee and sit there, gentle and inquisitive, giving an occasional squeak by way of conversation.

Outdoors, on her walks, her attention never strayed far from us, but she would let anyone approach her. If I decided to fly one of the buzzards and needed Pat's assistance, we'd put Jeannie on the ground and peg the end of her leash down. She would watch intently, following every move we made, never attempting to walk about as far as her leash would allow, never attempting to fly.

Only once did she ever display aggression and that, amazingly enough, was directed at Pat. It was one evening; we were going out. Upstairs, Pat got herself ready and put on her new wig. Wigs were all the rage then, and Pat had bought herself one as a bit of fun. Her own hair is long, dark brown and straight, she wears it loose or caught back in a pony-tail; the wig – a total change – was short, curly, and very blonde. She pinned it on and went downstairs, straight out to the car.

Later, when we returned, she never gave a thought to the wig. She busied herself doing various things, then made a cup of coffee and sat down to drink it. Jeannie always went through a to-do of greeting us when we entered the house, working her wings excitedly, weaving her body up and down and squeaking; she'd given me her usual enthusiastic welcome but rather made a point of ignoring Pat, who was too occupied to notice.

However, with her jobs attended to, she could sit down, put her feet up, drink her coffee and turn round to Jeannie, who was perched on the back of the chair. Pat said something to her, something inconsequential and affectionate, as she always did. This seemed to act as some kind of signal. Jeannie's huge claw shot out, snatched the wig and dragged it from Pat's head.

Pat yelled. She couldn't help it; she'd anchored the wig very firmly to her own hair and she felt she was being scalped. She was spilling hot coffee all over the place and trying, with her free hand, to do something about getting rid of Jeannie.

Hearing the yells, I rushed into the room and at once set about sorting out Pat, wig and bird. It wasn't easy. Jeannie gripped convulsively, her claws had become entangled in hair and she was twisting and snatching, trying to yank the wig from the pins that held it.

She won, she must have done, because she finished up with the wig while Pat clutched her head, wondering how much of her own hair she'd lost in the tussle. When she'd recovered she turned to Jeannie, who was standing on one leg, hugging the wig close to her chest and looking at Pat with her customary friendly air.

'Give it back to me,' Pat said calmly, holding out her hand. Jeannie relinquished it at once looking, as she did so, faintly puzzled to have had it in her possession at all.

Needless to say, Pat didn't put it back on, she didn't want to engage in another painful and undignified wrestling match, which she had no doubt would take place if she attempted to wear it again.

The cause – or causes – of Jeannie's behaviour could reasonably be guessed. The wig altered Pat's appearance considerably, and yet she went on *being* Pat. Recognising and yet

180

not recognising her, Jeannie had become utterly confused and taken aggressive measures to restore everything to normal. Or it could have seemed to her that some utterly strange animal was *sitting on Pat's head* – a circumstance dreadfully alarming, provoking a jealous hostility. Whatever accounted for Jeannie's attack one thing was certain, it wasn't a game. Unintentionally clumsy as she often was, all her games were gentle. Her picking up of objects from the floor was accomplished with an almost thoughtful delicacy, as if she had to take pains to treasure what she found; and her favourite game, with Pat's slippers, although it had its boisterous moments, was patient and amiable.

When Pat sat before the fire in the evening she would dangle one slipper from her toes. Jeannie, waiting, patrolled the floor with a controlled watchfulness, her eagerness gradually driving her to little hops of excitement. Backwards and forwards, circling, advancing and retreating, she somehow contained herself until Pat let the slipper drop, then she rushed forward to claim it.

Clutching her prize, she held it high up in one claw, hugging it to her chest, hopping one-legged about the room and squeaking delightedly. When she had savoured her triumph sufficiently she hopped into a corner and suddenly flung the slipper away.

Her aim was terrible. She frequently hit things, cats, people – sometimes other birds. But that never bothered her, crashing sounds had surrounded Jeannie practically from birth, they had become absorbed into her consciousness as merely an ingredient of daily life. Oblivious of any disturbance she caused she rushed after the slipper, retrieved it and was off again round the room, like a child playing hopscotch: round the furniture, in and out of the cats – whose expressions indicated they thought her no end of a fool – until it was time for the corner again, and another joyful hurl of the slipper.

One evening she played the game briefly, in a rather half-hearted way, then she took to her perch over the kitchen door until it was time for bed.

At bedtime, with everything and everyone downstairs – indoors and out – settled for the night, Jeannie fluttered from her perch. We were ready to go upstairs and she preceded us, making her hopping ascent, her wings spread out and brushing the walls on either side of the narrow staircase. About two from the top she'd give a sudden leap, impelling herself into the bedroom, where she'd fly around for a while and finally come to rest on top of the bedroom door. That was where she spent the night, every night, unmoving and silent, until daylight entered the room.

She always greeted us in the mornings when we woke, as if we'd been away for a very long time, but that morning her greeting was a little less exuberant than usual. During the course of the course of the day Pat noticed that she was holding one wing out a little, away from her body. She sat her on her knee and examined her carefully. All she could find was a small lump, scarcely bigger than a pea, on the joint of the wing, the inside of the elbow.

When I came home she pointed it out to me. It apparently caused Jeannie no pain, she didn't object at all when my fingers pressed against it; she just sat, so docile as to be almost dejected, while we examined her.

It seemed strange that such a tiny thing could account for the bird being off-colour, but we decided that must be the case. We spent the evening reading through our books and I found a somewhat inadequate reference that could fit the case. Hunting birds occasionally suffered from lumps; while no one stated definitely what caused them, the traditional opinion was that they were the result of the bird knocking itself. Iodine was prescribed; after a short treatment of this the lumps disappeared. As Jeannie was forever knocking herself it was a wonder she wasn't permanently covered in them. Relieved, I got out the first aid kit, full of old and new, bought, cadged and do-it-yourself remedies.

For two days we painted the lump with iodine. Jeannie was almost her normal self, eating as usual but rather quiet and always holding her wing out to one side. She didn't fly very much but there was nothing uncommon in that, she generally

182

preferred to walk, anyway. On the third morning, just before I left for work, she was on the bedroom door, squeaking persistently, asking to be brought downstairs.

It was much too early, she never came down until later in the morning; but Pat went up to see her, scolding her affectionately for being such a nuisance. She put up her hand and Jeannie hopped on to it. 'Listen, you know you can't come down yet. Go on the bed and look out of the window . . .' She carried Jeannie across the room and put her down on the bed.

Suddenly, there was blood.

There was so much blood Pat didn't know where it was coming from. Rich, horrifying, it gushed, spattering the bed, Pat's hand, the bird. Pat called, 'Jeannie's bleeding –' but I was already halfway up the stairs, having heard Pat's first, involuntary cry.

I picked Jeannie up and saw that the blood was apparently pumping from the tiny lump on her wing. I didn't have time to say anything, I simply took her in my hands, and in that instant her head flopped to one side. She was dead.

We couldn't believe it. Stunned by the suddenness of it we stood with blood on us, around us, spreading over the bedclothes, soaking into the bright plumage of the fishing hawk. From the first cry Pat had given to the moment Jeannie died, no more than forty seconds had passed.

Our house is small, it's crammed with sound and movement and its boundaries are the boundaries of our life; what happens in it is our own little world.

Jeannie altered that world. For the months of her illness our lives had revolved around caring for her and she had repaid us – if anyone ever thought in terms of repayment. Gentle, affectionate, playful, she took us as her own kind – as more than her own kind, giving back, in her need for us, everything we had given to her.

She never knew if she was a human being, or we were birds. Perhaps she thought we were all cats . . .

I had to go to work and Pat came to stand on the step to wave me off. Neither of us knew what to say; I murmured something about being busy and Pat nodded . . . yes, she must make a start, there was a great deal to do. There would always be a great deal to do: the telephone call, the knock on the door, the stranger in the porch saying, 'Can you help . . .'

But she lingered for a moment before going back in. It was very early in the morning, the streets were quiet. And in the house, in every room, a greater quietness still.